The
New Perennial
Garden

The
New Perennial
Garden

Noël Kingsbury

FRANCES LINCOLN

Frances Lincoln Limited
4 Torriano Mews
Torriano Avenue
London NW5 2RZ

British Library Cataloguing in Publication Data
A catalogue record for this book is available
from the British Library

ISBN 0 7112 1608 8

Printed and bound in Italy by New
Interlitho S.p.A.
First Frances Lincoln Edition 1996
First paperback edition 2000

9 8 7 6 5 4 3 2 1

HALF–TITLE PAGE *Hardy geraniums are excellent for flower and ground cover.*

FRONTISPIECE *A planting of naturally drought-tolerant perennials.*

RIGHT *A wildflower meadow in summer.*

Contents

In tune
with nature

A GARDEN IS A COMPROMISE BETWEEN nature and art. It is also a struggle between the two, between the instinct of nature to let plants grow, spread and compete with one another and the will of the gardener to keep everything in check, to make it conform to the human plan. Traditionally, gardens have tended towards human control, allowing little room for nature to extemporize. Now, however, increasing numbers of gardeners in many different countries are developing new styles of gardening which give nature more of a free rein.

A garden, perhaps more than anything else, should be a place to sit and relax. The new perennial garden offers town and country dwellers alike the opportunity to create a harmonious environment inspired by nature. Here, the magnificent grass Stipa gigantea *arches over varieties of day lily growing alongside pink phlox and red astilbe.*

In tune with nature

Gardening as conventionally practised can be an extraordinarily wasteful exercise, squandering both time and the earth's precious resources. This is partly because of the tendency to try to change the garden environment to suit the plant rather than to follow nature and grow what comes naturally. Why try to drain a damp patch of soil so as to grow bearded irises when a host of other irises will relish the moisture? Why keep adding peat to alkaline soils in order to grow rhododendrons when thousands of other shrubs will do much better with absolutely nothing added to the soil? Why nurse plants that are native to warmer climates for the sake of a couple of months' summer colour only to watch them die with the first frosts?

The irony of conventional gardening is that it involves so much destruction of the natural environment in a largely futile attempt to change the conditions prevailing in the garden. It is not just the destruction of peat bogs for peat or the plundering of the seas for fishmeal and seaweed soil conditioner, but also the falling water tables caused by the obsession with vast stretches of emerald-green lawns in dry areas, the tonnes of pollutants pumped into the air by lawnmowers and the mountains of waste plastic generated by the production of bedding plants. Simply choosing plants that thrive in the given conditions is one way to massively reduce damage to our environment. It also greatly reduces damage to your bank balance and your back.

Gardening in tune with nature involves selecting plants that not only thrive in the conditions of a particular garden but also coexist happily together, with relatively little need for the gardener to intervene, to stop one species swamping another, for instance. It is this creation of plant communities, artificial versions of natural ecosystems, that makes this style of gardening so new. It is low-maintenance because it does not set out to defy nature but to work with and understand natural processes. If a planting in a garden is far removed from what would occur there naturally – for example, the rhododendron on a limey soil or a bed of half-hardy plants in an area prone to frosts – then it will be very unstable. A lot of input in the form of labour, chemicals and so on will be needed to stop this artificial state of affairs from collapsing under the pressure of the environment – the rhododendrons dying from iron deficiency or a late spring frost killing the half-hardy bedding plants. Gardening in tune with nature involves a process of meeting nature halfway, to create gardens that are made up of relatively stable plant communities – stable because they are appropriate to the local environment.

Once established, this kind of planting requires substantially less work than conventional borders. In many cases only once-a-year cutting or strimming is called for. This makes it attractive for anyone who wants to reduce the workload in their gardens or has little time to garden – people with second homes, for example.

The appearance of these plantings is very often dramatically different from conventional plantings; wilder and more naturalistic, certainly, but also more romantic. They are ideal for gardeners who value closeness to nature or who want to bring the natural world to urban or suburban environments. Of course, neatly manicured grass and regimented borders will always appeal to some tastes, to whom tall meadow grass and wildflowers can seem untidy and uncared for. Opinions are shifting, though, as increasing numbers of the public and private bodies that are responsible for managing our urban environments are encouraging a more natural look in public spaces.

A garden in tune with nature can be a major resource for local wildlife, from insects and other invertebrates to the reptiles, amphibians, mammals and birds that feed on them. It is the possibility of creating one's own nature reserve, a private link in the food chain, that attracts many people to the idea of the natural garden. A well-planned choice of food plants, shelter and water will foster constant wildlife interest through the seasons – birds nesting among flowering shrubs in spring, a pond buzzing with insect and amphibian life and bordered by colourful flowers in summer, flocks of migratory birds feeding on berries and seedheads in autumn and winter. Indeed, for people whose main gardening interest is encouraging wildlife rather than growing ornamental plants, the new style of gardening offers a chance not only to develop the wildlife potential of the garden but at the same time to make it more attractive to people.

'Enhanced nature' is a good description of what the new perennial garden tries to achieve. This dry soil planting, in which the bright colours of cerise Lychnis coronaria *and violet salvias stand out, is a freer interpretation of the traditional border.*

Plant communities in nature

For us to be able to create successful naturalistic plantings in the garden it is necessary to have some understanding of how plants behave in nature. Plants in the wild are to a greater or lesser extent tied to their environment, and climate is the over-riding factor that governs plant growth. Latitude – how far north or south you are between the steamy equator and the icy poles – is a starting point from which to understand climate, although this is modi-fied by landmass and by altitude. The same sort of 'Mediterranean-climate' plants will grow around San Francisco as around Lisbon, both roughly 38°N and both with weather conditions influenced by an ocean to the west. The number of these plants that can be grown inland is limited because of the far greater winter cold; the general rule is that the larger the landmass, the more extreme the climate will be at its centre. In the North American continent St Louis, for example – on the same latitude as San Francisco – has bitter winters that virtually rule out Mediterranean plants, although they could tolerate its hot summers. The southwest tip of Scotland, at 56°N, has an unusually mild climate because it is warm-ed by the balmy Gulf Stream; Moscow, a few thousand kilometres due east, has the classic continental extremes of cold winters and hot, dry summers. The effect of altitude is that the higher you go, the colder it becomes. A walk in a mountainous region illustrates this well. It is possible to start among vineyards on sunny, sheltered slopes and end your hike in patches of snow only a few hours later.

Similar, if less dramatic, effects can be seen nearer home as the broad effects of climate are modified locally by the lie of the land. A disused quarry will demonstrate how different sorts of vegetation colonize slopes in sun and shade, or moist and dry areas. Subtler changes can be seen on a walk through an undulating field where there are moister and drier patches, each with its own different vegetation.

Given the existence of certain conditions within a particular geographical region – soil type, moisture, light, aspect and so on – ecologists are able to predict what kinds of vegetation are likely to be found growing together there in a plant community. For instance, in open areas with a sufficient depth of soil you will tend to find grassland. What species of grass, and the extent to which they are mixed with broad-leaved plants, depends partly on natural factors such as soil chemistry and moisture, but also on human considerations such as how the site is managed – whether it is grazed, for example.

Some plants are more tolerant and adapt-able than others. Meadow buttercups (*Ranunculus acris*), for example, can be found on a wide range of soils in sunny meadow situations, whereas the devil's-bit scabious (*Succisa pratensis*) has more stringent ecological needs and can only be found on rather infertile, damp ground, usually where there is grazing. Both these are grassland species, but each favours a slightly different ecological niche.

Within a plant community each plant has a particular role. Some may cover extensive areas of ground, others will appear as isolated specimens. Some will flower early and die down, to be succeeded in their place by others later in the year, and so on.

A plant community is stable in the short term, and we rarely see dramatic changes from one year to the next. In the long term, however, development is often going on. The natural succession in a temperate climate can be seen if we picture what happens when a garden is abandoned. Grass usually takes over fairly rapidly at first, along with a few robust wildflowers, but after several years the grass-based plant community becomes invaded by brambles and scrub, often hawthorn and birch. Eventually these taller plants cast increasing shade, in which the grass is unable to survive. By then oak, beech and ash seedlings may well have found their way into the scrub. Since they grow taller still, they will eventually shade out the hawthorn and birch. An oak/beech forest would be the most stable plant community in this area, the one to which this land would eventually return if left untended. In other regions other types of stable plant community, usually tree-dominated, would develop; ecologists call these 'climatic climax' communities. It is usually only human activities such as farming and gardening that stop this inevitable march towards the re-establish-ment of climax vegetation.

So plant communities do alter slowly over time; even in the oak and beech forest there is change. As old trees die and fall over, light is let through to the forest floor, which permits the rapid growth of foxgloves (*Digitalis purpurea*), and then bluebells (*Hyacinthoides non-scripta*), red campion (*Silene dioica*) and deadnettles (*Lamium* species). This plant community thrives for maybe ten to twenty years before seedling trees close up the forest canopy once more.

Many of the theoretically unstable plant communities survive because there is some factor – sometimes natural, more often human – that keeps on thwarting the tree community that would naturally displace them. By destroying trees, fire keeps many areas of moorland under heather (which regenerates after burning); fire was also the mechanism that kept much of the American prairie from turning into woodland. Simi-

larly, by eliminating woody plants at seedling stage, the constant munching of cattle –
and the annual mowing of meadows –
ensures the survival of pastureland as grass.

Plant survival strategies

A knowledge of how plants survive in the
wild can be a great help in understanding
how they can be selected for use in the
garden. Plant ecologists talk of three
categories: competitors, stress tolerators and
disturbance tolerators.

Competitors are vigorous species that can
make the most of good conditions for
growth – plentiful moisture and nutrients
and an equable climate. They include species that gain advantage over their fellows
by height or by being mobile, quickly able
to send new shoots into neighbouring vacant
territory. Vigorous meadow grasses and fast-
growing perennials like hardy geraniums
and goldenrod are examples.

Stress tolerators are those that flourish in
difficult conditions – shade, drought, poor
soils, harsh climates. They grow slowly but
can survive bad times in a way that the
competitors usually cannot. They include
plants like wild thyme, able to withstand
poor, dry soils, and thrift, adapted to make
the most of minimal soil and salt winds.

Disturbance tolerators are opportunists
that make the most of bare areas of soil –
molehills, animal activity, fallen trees, fire
damage, erosion and human disturbance
(such as digging a flower bed). Many are
fast-growing annuals or short-lived perennials, which flower and seed rapidly before
they are displaced by other more permanent
competitor species taking over the newly
available site. Many survive over the years in
the form of buried seed, able to germinate
rapidly when soil disturbance brings it to the
surface. Field poppies (*Papaver rhoeas*) are a
colourful example in open habitats, foxgloves in partially shaded ones.

*Natural or traditionally managed
environments, such as this Austrian hay
meadow, offer inspiration for our own
gardening. Here buttercups and* Geranium
sylvaticum *cover large areas in early
summer. Creating a similar spectacle on a
small scale involves carefully matching plants
with the environment.*

Plant communities in the garden

WE HAVE JUST SEEN HOW PLANT communities in the wild are stable in the short term but change slowly over the years. The first stages of this change seem rapid in the context of a garden that ceases to be tended. Conventional gardens are extremely vulnerable: the lawn invades the borders and weeds, grasses and the more vigorous garden plants take over any bare soil until, in just a year or two, the garden becomes completely overgrown. Allowing the natural succession of plant communities to run its course unchecked is not what natural gardening or even wild gardening is about. Our aim is to explore ways of making gardens that are far more stable, to find ways of planting that minimize the tasks of weeding, watering, mowing and pruning, and which are more resistant to invasion by weeds. Of course, some maintenance is always going to be necessary if the land is not to start on the long road to reverting to forest, and also to ensure that an attractive mix of species flourishes.

The next time that you go for a walk in the country, look at the plants around you and compare the way that they grow with how plants are grown in gardens. For one thing there is no bare earth, at least not in open habitats: nature abhors a vacuum, and there will always be some plant seeding itself or encroaching on any bare soil. And then there is the way that plants grow together and mingle haphazardly. In a garden, plants are usually grown as discrete individuals, separate clumps or as blocks of a single species. In the wild, different species blend together. In a meadow, for example, a mixture of grasses takes up most of the space, but exploiting tiny pockets of ground

between them are wildflowers. Some of these lean on the grasses for support, or even climb up them, while others have rosettes of leaves at ground level sending up taller flower spikes. In such communities, plants use up every available bit of ground, which presents quite a contrast to the arrangement in a conventional garden.

If we want to create a garden based on natural plantings, it is important that we choose not just individual plants but a whole plant community. These should be plants that are closely matched ecologically to the environment so that they flourish with minimum encouragement, are growing vigorously and intermingling to use up all available space so that they deny a place to invasive weeds. It is important to think in terms of a plant community because compatible plants growing together as they do in nature need less maintenance than when conventionally planted in gardens where individuals are put together on an aesthetic rather than an ecological basis.

The most reliable plant communities to try are ones based on wild communities, those that are known to be stable in their preferred habitat and are native to your region. These can be enhanced with a selection of plants from other regions that have similar ecological needs, perhaps relatives of the native species that will add extra colour or lengthen the season of flower. There is, of course, nothing to stop adventurous gardeners from making up their own plant communities, and although the results will be less easy to predict, they will rarely be unattractive.

Plants vary in how competitive they are, and much of the work of any gardener is spent in ensuring that strong growers do not smother weaker ones. Some environments (like fertile soils) favour vigorous plants; others (such as poor dry soils) favour

slower-growing, but more stress-tolerant, species. By choosing plants on an ecological basis – matching them closely to prevailing conditions – you should find that the majority will be of roughly similar competitiveness. Garden plant communities always work best when the plants that make them up are of approximately equal vigour.

Weeds

All weeds are wildflowers, of course, but it is customary to define them as undesirable when they compete with the more attractive plants that we try to cultivate. Weeds come in two main categories. *Strong competitors*, like nettles, couch grass and dock, are perennial. Some have persistent tap roots that are hard to eradicate; others rapidly spread, with running root systems that give rise to new plants. *Disturbance tolerators*, like groundsel and willow herb, are usually annuals. They are opportunists that germinate rapidly on bare ground but rarely survive for more than a year (though they do seed prolifically during that brief life if allowed to flower.) The conventional garden, with its expanses of bare soil, is the perfect habitat for disturbance tolerators. It is little wonder that it involves so much maintenance, especially the hoeing and forking out of newly germinating weed seedlings.

Establishing plant communities does involve quite a bit of work, as there will be competition from weeds until the plants are mature enough and intermingled enough to exclude them. Perennial competitor weeds are the worst problem, as failure to get rid of every scrap of root completely at the out-set will mean that new plants will sprout and start to infiltrate a planting. Disturbance tolerators are less troublesome, because once a perennial plant community is up and running their habitat will rapidly vanish and they will be forced out.

Slightly acid humus-rich soils, such as are found in established woodland, are the ideal environment for some of the most attractive shade-loving plants, most of which are spring-flowering. Here drifts of blue, white and pink creeping phlox (Phlox stolonifera) *consort with the foamy cream heads of a tiarella species and the blue hanging clusters of* Mertensia pulmonarioides (*syn.* M. virginica). *Ferns will flourish too, especially if the site is moist; these are* Matteuccia struthiopteris *and on the right the evergreen fern* Polystichum acrostichoides.

New styles of gardening

By LOOKING TO NATURE FOR INSPIRATION, the new perennial gardener seeks to enrich our surroundings — creating a natural haven in built-up areas, and making a positive contribution to the environment in the country. As with any garden, it has to fulfil many functions. It should look beautiful in itself and fit appropriately into its context; it should provide amenities that the whole family can use; the time and effort needed to manage it should be geared to what you can comfortably spare, and it should play a worthwhile part in the local ecosystem.

Consider some of the forms that a design based on perennial planting can take, then work out how they might fit into your plot, and whether they would suit your tastes and your gardening priorities.

There is no denying the romance of the new perennial garden. Soft colours, a range of flower shapes and blending of varieties produce an effect that is both natural and artistic. Yellow goldenrods and yarrow predominate, with the tall plumes of macleaya and the mauve veronica adding pastel shades to the planting.

Some of the new ways of planting perennials offer alternatives to what in a conventional garden would be a functional lawn or an ornamental flower bed or border. Others provide solutions to 'problem areas' such as slopes or boggy ground. Take a closer look at the characteristics of the main options to help you decide whether they are appropriate for you and your garden.

Wildflower lawns

A wildflower lawn comes somewhere between conventional mown grass and a full-blown wildflower meadow. Compact, bright wildflowers like daisies (*Bellis perennis*), self-heal (*Prunella vulgaris*) and hawkbit (*Leontodon hispidus*) spatter the surface with spots of colour, but the turf is short enough to walk and play on, and for the varied uses to which families normally put lawns, although it will not take very heavy wear and tear. (In this case you could run a line of stepping stones through the lawn to cope with a route where traffic is particularly intense.)

A wildflower lawn is a good alternative to a wildflower meadow in a small garden because it looks relatively tidy, which makes it suitable for high-visibility areas. Where part of a larger garden is given over to wildflower meadow, wildflower lawn makes an excellent treatment for the foreground, and forms paths through the longer grass.

Besides needing less attention than conventional lawns, a great advantage of wildflower lawns is that they can succeed on a wide range of soils. By planting bulbs such as crocuses that happily naturalize in grass, the lawn can be a sea of colour in spring, with the peak of its perennial flowering in early summer.

Wildflower meadows

This is the wild-garden style *par excellence*. When well done it creates a wonderfully romantic haze of colourful wildflowers blooming amid a variety of grasses. When not so successful it is a rather untidy mass of dull grass interspersed with docks and other undesirable wildflowers. The best meadows tend to be on poorer soils, where the stronger-growing grasses and competitive weeds do less well. However, with good plant selection and well-timed mowing, a reasonably attractive and tidy meadow can be created on most soils.

A meadow is almost by definition a large, open tract of land, so this style needs a reasonable amount of space. Meadows seem a natural part of the country garden. When carefully designed to include a high proportion of colourful flowering plants and well managed, there is no reason why they should not feature more frequently in urban environments, taking the place of a conventional border or lawn. After all, they bring a note of rural tranquillity to soulless built-up areas and can play an important role in attracting wildlife back to the city. Furthermore, they involve little main-tenance once established. This makes the treatment particularly useful for banks and slopes where cutting conventional short grass is difficult.

Prairies

Where the soil is fertile and grasses grow vigorously, it makes sense to look to the American prairies for inspiration, where large robust perennials are used *en masse*. Many prairie perennials such as bergamot (*Monarda*), goldenrod (*Solidago*) and black-eyed Susan (*Rudbeckia*) have been popular as border plants for over a hundred years. Unlike many smaller wildflowers, the majority of prairie species will grow on fertile soils, competing well with vigorous grasses. The majority of prairie plants begin to look their best from midsummer on, with a peak of flowering in late summer, when majestic Joe Pye weed (*Eupatorium*), rudbeckias and ironweeds (*Vernonia*) bloom at head-height among swaying grasses. The seedheads of these plants are attractive in their own right during the winter months. The purist can grow a prairie consisting entirely of species native to the American Midwest – a selection of plants unrivalled for their ability to survive intensely cold winters and hot summers. Most of us may well want a more pragmatic version of a prairie, combining locally common grass species with robust perennials chosen from a range of sources, garden varieties as well as species.

Prairie effects are obviously most dramatic when done on a large scale, but could be adapted for a smaller bed.

Open borders

I use this term to describe plantings that resemble the traditional border in many ways, but do without the backdrop of wall, fence or hedge that borders often rely on. Conventionally, gardens have tended to be dominated by lawn, with planting restricted to the outer boundaries of the garden or dotted around in island beds. Many gardeners, especially keen growers of perennial plants, are experimenting with a much wider conception of herbaceous planting, growing the plants in broad drifts, with narrow paths cutting through them, often replacing areas of lawn. Unlike a wildflower meadow or prairie, there is no grass matrix, although ornamental grasses are frequently incorporated in the mixture. Such plantings can be supremely colourful, especially during the summer, and they tend to enjoy wider public acceptance than meadows. How much maintenance they need depends on the types of plant chosen. If you choose simple species plants and cultivars and hybrids that are still close in character to wild species, planting them so

that an absolute minimum of bare earth is
exposed, then attention can be kept to a
minimum.

Ponds and wetland

Water features combine a focus of interest
with a valuable refuge for local wildlife.
The margins of natural pools provide a
habitat for plants that tolerate waterlogging
or enjoy moisture at the roots, so position-
ing a purpose-made pond beside an area
planted up with moisture-lovers creates an
appropriate garden setting. Where there is a
drainage problem, this can be the most
sensible use of the damp ground. Moisture-
loving plants are generally strong growers,
with a tendency to flower in the summer
rather than in spring.

Dry-land plantings

Many gardens, not just those in regions that
experience hot dry summers, have an area
with thin or poor soil that dries quickly. A
bank facing the sun with sparse topsoil over
the underlying rock is quite a common
situation in which the majority of garden
plants struggle for survival, and
maintenance can be difficult. Using low
shrubs, bulbs such as *Tulipa* species and
drought-resistant perennials native to areas
of dry summers, it is possible to create
attractive plantings that need little
attention. Flowering will be at its peak in
early summer, but since many of these
subjects are evergreen, the area will look
good all year round.

　Similar planting works for the sharp
drainage of natural scree gardens and
patches of gravel such as little-used paths.

*Paths mown through long grass create an air
of romantic softness and bring the
atmosphere of meadow and countryside right
into the garden.*

Choosing a style

A GARDEN INSPIRED BY NATURE need not look wild. The approaches to planting that we have just looked at provide scope for developing gardens varying in style from the relatively trim to the outrageously jungly. The degree of wildness is partly due to the influence of the soil on the plants chosen, but is largely the result of how the planting is managed and presented. Fertile, moist soils encourage lush growth among the already vigorous plant species that favour them, often resulting in vegetation that becomes excessively rank, especially towards the end of the season. Unless you

garden on a large scale and enjoy this kind of exuberance, it is best to restrict such plantings to well defined beds or particular areas of the garden. You can do something towards managing grass-based habitats like meadows by an appropriate mowing routine, and even tall prairie plants can be made to submit to a more respectable suburban regime by cutting until midsummer, then leaving until winter. They will grow and flower, but at a reduced height compared to what they would do normally. Poor, dry soils, on the other hand, favour tighter-growing plants with a sparser and neater habit – making it easier for the gardener to keep a planting layout in good shape.

It is often possible to exploit such

differences even in a small site to create the satisfying contrasts of scale and texture that make a garden interesting. Many people like to have a relatively tidy zone near the house, the high-visibility area seen initially by visitors and passers by, and to allow increasingly relaxed and exuberant behaviour among plants as distance increases. The majority of gardeners also want areas seen from the house to look as ornamental for as much of the year as possible. Apart from the need to present a pleasing face to the world, practicalities to be catered for may include children's play, summer games and entertaining – as well as paths for access and areas of hard standing. All this need not necessarily be at odds with natural planting.

Wildflower lawns are the obvious alternative to the conventional lawn, combining tidiness, practicality and interest. Wide sweeps of perennial planting in 'open borders' look highly ornamental, ideal for informal high-visibility areas. Perhaps the most effective kind of planting for such areas, and lowest-maintenance of all, is the gravel garden. Here dryland plants such as lavenders and wild herbs like oregano, thyme and sage are grown in soil overlain by a layer of gravel. A mellow shade of stone can set the plants off beautifully, and it is difficult for weed seedlings to gain a foothold. At the same time, a certain amount of foot traffic can be accommodated. Such schemes are suitable for both small and large gardens.

Once away from the pressure of maintaining high-visibility orderliness around the house, it is possible to step up the degree of wildness. At the outer edges of the garden

Giving plants such as sweet rocket or dame's violet (Hesperis matronalis) *the liberty to self-seed is one way of developing a more naturalistic style.*

robust perennials, wildflowers and grass can be allowed to grow as tall as they like with only minimal mowing, perhaps just once a year. Such quieter and less frequented parts of the garden will be the areas of most interest to visiting wildlife, birds especially.

Many gardens have separate front and back areas. Traditionally the front has been for show and the back for recreation or functional purposes such as vegetable growing. Often, especially in suburban areas, the front garden is kept as lawn with only limited planting, but the new generation of perennial gardeners is discovering that it has a lot more potential. Why not plant up the whole area as an 'open border', with low-growing and colourful perennials filling the space, and narrow paths wending through for viewing the plants and for maintenance? This kind of planting is similar to the 'cottage garden' style that has become very popular in recent decades, similarly relying on informal and intermingled planting of perennials.

A wilder style of natural garden feature – such as wildflower meadows, prairie plantings or informal borders of large perennials – can look acceptably tidy by being made to seem planned and intended, rather than having the air of a planting 'gone to seed'. Just as neatly edged lawns bring the right sharpness of focus to a formal layout, so the use of framing devices helps to keep massed plants in their place as part of a garden composition. A prairie or meadow area edged with borders of mown grass and traversed by similarly mown paths has an impact that is quite different from the effect of a solid mass of long grass and wildflowers.

No lawn of conventionally shaved grass can compete with a wildflower meadow like this. Mowing, feeding and many other maintenance operations are reduced, too.

The garden framework

WOODY PLANTS, TREES AND SHRUBS play an essential part in dictating the structural framework of a garden. So, too, to a lesser and more seasonal extent, do tall perennials and grasses. They all control space by closing off some areas of vision and accentuating others. They can be used to create areas of privacy and seclusion, to be appreciated by adults in search of tranquillity, by children in pursuit of a stage for imaginative games, and by wildlife for safe roosting and nesting places. Trees and shrubs can also separate different parts of the garden, each with its own character. Such a division offers one way of combining both natural informality and a more formal area within one garden. However, combining naturalistic planting alongside

formality can be effective too, sparking that feeling of 'creative tension' that marks many great works of art. We have already noted how mown surrounds bring 'wild' planting into focus. Similar framing devices could be created with decking, or even low clipped hedges. Another kind of contrast is to introduce formal elements such as ornaments, urns or the occasional clipped yew or box. Carefully positioned, sculptural focal points and punctuating geometrical shapes bring a note of formality to remind us that this is indeed a garden and to contrast powerfully with the carefree growth of the wildflowers.

Informal planting can also sit happily with conventional borders. A particular trick that works well is to have wildflower meadow separated from a border by a narrow mown path, so that from only a short distance away it seems as if the border merges romantically with the grass. Planting around terraces and other seating

areas needs to be carefully planned. This is where people most appreciate a long season of colour and fragrance, as well as garden features that offer visual interest, and you may like to include a selection of more exotic species to enhance your perennial mixture. Pools always provide interesting focal points, and where the soil is appropriately damp the luxuriant waterside vegetation can be taken a stage further by the addition of a few large-leaved species for spectacular effects – rodgersias, the giant rhubarb *Gunnera manicata*, the giant reed *Arundo donax* and so on. Such large plants are well able to look after themselves once established.

Where the soil is dry, the opposite effect might be obtained around a terrace, creating a more Mediterranean look with grey-leaved shrubs, wild herbs and – for added impact – dryland plants with strongly 'architectural' foliage such as yuccas or cardoon (*Cynara cardunculus*). Such a

LEFT *Long grass and wildflowers (here cowslips,* Primula veris*) can work well visually in the midst of more conventional gardens. This particular area is mown after the cowslips seed, in early summer, and becomes a tidy lawn the rest of the year. Clipped shapes, such as the shrub in the background, and mown paths, enhance the feeling that the longer grass is intentional and not laziness.*

RIGHT *A neatly clipped formal hedge provides a solid framework for a harmonious late summer blend of interlaced foliage and flower, including yellow coreopsis, pink salvias and mauve* Verbena bonariensis. *The tall spires of mullein can provide useful vertical features in any space, however small, while just beyond, the huge silver* Onopordum acanthium *is a magnificent stage setter for larger gardens.*

planting can be not only an imaginative use of the poor-quality infertile soil often found around houses, but an appropriate one for enhancing a warm summer atmosphere on a terrace. Even if the soil is not dry, an emphasis on ground-hugging shrubs like lavenders, cistus and rock roses (*Helianthemum*) will help to create such an atmosphere.

Traditional bedding may not seem an obvious candidate to combine with the new perennial planting, but it can be done. Intensely coloured late-summer perennials such as rudbeckias and other 'daisies' can be mixed with cheerful annuals such as marigolds and zinnias, or soft-textured grasses like miscanthus or *Molinia caerulea* with lax annuals like cosmos or sweet peas.

The fact that annuals and bedding plants are normally seen in formal situations should not put us off using them, but we should be experimenting with different and more informal arrangements.

Our observations from country walks of how and where plants grow can be put into practice in our treatment of garden boundaries and any vertical features such as pergolas and summer houses. Climbers clamber over shrubs and up trees in nature, yet how often is this seen in the garden, where they are nearly always neatly tied to a trellis? Allowing them freedom to cloak man-made structures such as fences and walls and clothe slopes creates an extra dimension of wildness. Climbers can not only achieve effective camouflage but extend

seasons of interest; when summer-flowering climbers are encouraged to sprawl over spring-flowering shrubs or trees, or to decorate evergreens that are part of the winter framework, the same space is effectively used twice over.

Creating a garden inspired by nature is one way in which the urban dweller can escape from the concrete jungle. A wild-flower lawn, some wildflowers mixed in with garden plants, a tiny pond and lots of climbers scrambling luxuriantly up all available vertical surfaces can make all the difference. The ideal perhaps is that the city can be hidden from view by vegetation, but another tactic is to make the attractions of a natural garden so engrossing that the eye does not seek to stray beyond them.

Lessons from nature

Choosing the plant species that grow well naturally is the practical key to this kind of gardening. Our efforts should go into finding the plants that will succeed in our conditions, rather than trying to change the conditions to grow plants unsuited to local soil and climate. First we need to consider the factors that affect plant growth. This will help us see how plants will behave in the conditions we are able to offer them.

Light and plant growth

A cursory glance at plants growing under trees and in the open reveals many obvious differences. Under trees there are few, if any, grasses and few tall perennials. Instead you find more low-growing plants, many with dark evergreen leaves, and the vegetation is relatively sparse. The deeper the shade, the thinner the plant cover becomes. Most flowers are to be seen in the spring, with

little or nothing appearing later on. Light plays a crucial role in determining which species will grow in a given place. Those that favour light, open habitats are generally much more competitive than those in shadier habitats, because they can utilize the sun's energy and other resources to grow bigger and spread faster. Shade-tolerant plants are slower and smaller, but can often utilize low light levels better — through being evergreen, for instance (like hellebores), or by doing most of their active growth at times when the trees overhead are without leaves (like wood anemone, *Anemone nemorosa*). Most sun-lovers do poorly if planted in shade, while shade-lovers can get scorched in full sun.

Water and plant growth

We all know that plants need water and suffer quickly if they go short. Some need a lot more than others, though, and it is vitally important to match the moisture level of your garden with appropriate species. The difference between drought-tolerant and moisture-loving plants is even more dramatic than that between sun- and

shade-lovers. Many plants from dry climates have a 'dry' look; they have compact, wiry stems bearing small, greyish leaves which have evolved particular shapes and textures to withstand the sun's scorching and minimize water loss; other dry-climate plants are succulent, storing moisture in specially adapted cells. Plants from moist habitats, on the other hand, can afford large leaves and fleshy stems and tend to look lush and rather exuberant.

Abundant water enables the majority of plants to grow rapidly. Strong-growing, competitive species are thus at a great advantage on damp ground; indeed, they are liable to elbow slower-growers and plants less able to tolerate waterlogging out of the way. The exception is when poor drainage occurs on very poor acid soils. The plants that grow in these boggy conditions form a very specialized, but fascinating, community.

Soils and plant growth

On the whole most plant species will grow well on a wide variety of soils. When they exhibit a preference for a particular soil it is often because of some other factor that is associated with the soil type, rather than the soil itself. Soil is an immensely complicated subject, but a number of generalizations can be made to give guidance in plant selection.

Sandy soils hold neither moisture nor nutrients well, so tend to be dry and poor. If the experience of gardening neighbours indicates that many popular garden plants do not thrive, it may be best to concentrate on the stress-tolerant plant communities we look at on pages 96-7. Such plants have the

A natural planting in a boggy wildflower meadow shows how effective a limited palette of colours can be. Magenta Cirsium heterophyllum *might be overpowering in a clump, but blends well with a very pale pink valerian and neutral colours.*

advantage of being able to cope with conditions which faster-growing plants find difficult. You will not miss out; many of them are very colourful and they include a good number of evergreens.

Clay soils are not wet by nature, but if there is any problem with drainage, they can become waterlogged very easily. Clay soils are so difficult to work that they have gained an undeservedly bad reputation. Since for our purposes we are interested not in endlessly tilling the soil to grow vegetables or annuals, but in permanent perennial plantings, this need not really concern us. We are much more able to appreciate their advantages – especially their fertility, which is a boon for the lover of the larger and more vigorous perennials.

Soils vary greatly in their chemistry, but the overriding question for gardeners is whether they are alkaline (limey, calcareous) or acid. The answer (easily ascertained with a pH testing kit, available from garden centres) will have a major effect on plant choice, and hence on the ultimate appearance of a garden.

An acid soil is generally poor, but supports the Ericaceae, the immensely large and varied heather family, and a great many other fine shrubs from different parts of the world. Relatively few herbaceous perennials thrive, so the natural gardener needs to concentrate on a variety of shrubs, which could include many of the low-growing heathers and rhododendrons, and certain grasses from moorland habitats. The potential is vast, so although the ambience of a garden on such a soil may reflect the heathland origin of many of the plants, it need not feel bleak or barren. With suitable moisture and shade, certain ferns and plants of woodland origin – including some lily species, trilliums and so on – can be added.

A slightly alkaline soil, or a neutral one, is generally more fertile and far more suitable

for herbaceous perennials. (A soil containing lime, however, is anathema to many shrubs that do well on acid soils.) A garden on such a soil can be built around borders, wildflower meadows and other plantings that use vigorous perennials and grasses, interspersed with those shrubs and climbers – clematis, for example – that flourish in these conditions. Fertility brings its own problems, the growth of weeds being one. Concentrating on a thick cover of strongly competitive plants will ensure that weeds get little chance to take over. Fortunately most popular herbaceous perennials fall into the competitive category.

A thin soil over limestone or chalk will be seen by many as a problem soil – thin, dry and relatively infertile. However, some of

Blending varieties that like similar conditions and letting plants grow in natural drifts can produce beautifully harmonious plantings. Here, pink monarda and sidalcea weave amongst a silver-leaved artemisia.

the most exciting and beautiful of all wildflowers are to be found on these soils. Small-growing but stress-tolerant wildflowers, some popular as 'rockery' or 'alpine' plants, thrive in these circumstances, whereas the vigorous-growing species, including many weeds, are unable to find the resources they need to grow well. Consequently a thin limestone soil can be remarkably rewarding, giving you the opportunity to grow a choice range of plants, including the perfect wildflower lawn.

Dry environments can be spectacularly colourful in early summer. The plants growing here all thrive in drought conditions and on poor soils. Yellow Asphodeline liburnica *grows among mats of a pale purple nepeta, with dark pink* Dianthus carthusianorum, *the darker, dense heads of* Allium sphaerocephalon, *and the pale thistle-like heads of an eryngium.*

25

Encouraging wildlife

ONE REASON FOR GARDENERS to turn to a more natural style of gardening is to attract and benefit a variety of wild animal species.

Wild creatures, whether invertebrates or higher animals such as mammals and birds, need food supplies and places to rest or hibernate where they are safe from predators and similarly safe places to breed. To ensure a good food supply for as wide a range of fauna as possible it is important that a long stretch of the food chain is incorporated. It is no good providing nesting boxes for birds if there is nothing nearby for them to eat while they are incubating and feeding their young. Besides food plants, habitats need to be provided for a whole range of invertebrates that we might be unaware of ourselves but which are a vital part of the diet of the animals in the garden.

When it comes to supplying these essential needs the key word is diversity, both of species and of habitats. Grass kept mown to different levels provides habitats for different insects, while shrubs and climbers of different kinds provide roosting and nesting sites for a variety of birds. Many insects – especially the larvae – are very particular about which plants they eat; the dependence of red admiral butterflies on stinging nettles (*Urtica dioica*) and of monarchs on butterfly weed (*Asclepias*

A pond with moisture-loving plants around its margins is a solution to the problem of badly drained ground. This decorative feature is a rich resource for wildlife.

tuberosa) are well known examples. It is important not only to provide a wide variety of plants, but particularly of native species, as introduced plants do not support anything like as many kinds of insect. Certain plants are much more important as food sources than others. For example in Europe the common oak (*Quercus robur*) supports hundreds of species, while the beech (*Fagus sylvatica*) supports a good deal fewer; introduced American oaks, in contrast, provide food for hardly any native European insects. However, this does not mean that wildlife gardening dictates a 'natives only' policy. Many animals are not at all particular and feeding them means that we plant the best food sources, wherever they may be from. Serviceberries – species of *Amelanchier* – from North America are among the best berry sources that anyone anywhere can plant to feed birds through the winter, and *Buddleja davidii* from China is likewise unbeatable for attracting butterflies. To some extent the gardener can make up for deficiences in the local wild flora by growing introduced species. Northern Europe, for instance, has relatively few nectar sources for insects from late summer to spring. The cultivation of late-flowering North American asters and goldenrods can make a lot of difference to butterfly populations, while the winter-flowering *Viburnum tinus* – native to the Mediterranean, but hardy in colder areas – feeds the insects around at that time.

Of all the things that a gardener can do to provide habitats, perhaps the best is to build a pond, preferably one with a slope to allow creatures access to the water and an appropriate range of aquatic, emergent and marginal plants. Within a surprisingly short

period of time water-dwelling insects and amphibians such as frogs will appear, even in the middle of a city. Pondlife is not only remarkably rich, but is also an endless (and educational) source of interest to children. Ponds and associated wetland areas offer yet another habitat for insects to breed. Although some of these might occasionally be a nuisance, they constitute another valuable link in the food chain.

Garden management can make a crucial difference to fauna. A tidy garden is an unnatural garden, denying shelter and food to a large number of creatures, and because it is an unnatural situation, it can actually be unhealthy, too! Honey fungus, a devastating threat to trees, thrives in neat parkland and gardens where all rotting wood is systematically cleared away. Where rotting wood remains, it encourages other fungi that parasitize and therefore restrain the growth of honey fungus. Piles of wood also feed a host of invertebrates such as woodlice, and can be used as hibernation places by reptiles, amphibians and small mammals such as hedgehogs. Clearing up too assiduously inevitably deprives some creature of a meal; grasses and perennials cut down in autumn, for instance, will feed no finches or other seed-eating birds.

A wildlife-friendly garden does not have to be unattractively untidy. Woodpiles and nettles can usually be tucked away in the outer reaches of the garden, and uncut perennials can be attractive in their own right, especially if some decorative species such as teasels (*Dipsacus fullonum*) and globe thistle (*Echinops*) are included.

Flowers and berries are important food sources. Berries (top right), like those of the climber Ampelopsis brevipedunculata *, are often vital for birds in winter. Tight clusters of small flowers (right) such as this* Sedum spectabile *are useful for butterflies.*

Selecting plants

THE ATTRACTION OF GARDENS inspired by nature is precisely that they resemble nature, or at least a perfected or idealized version of it. One important factor is the choice of plants that are naturally beautiful, not the double or oversized flowers and garish colours of a conventionally showy garden. These not only look forced and artificial in a natural-style setting, but the additional care and fuss they demand also make them unsuitable. For example, highly bred flowers with extra-large blooms often need stakes for support, which creates more work for the gardener and a less natural effect in the garden.

Purists will perhaps want to stick to naturally occurring species, but most of us will be more flexible in our choice of plants. Taking wildflowers as our inspiration, we will be prepared to augment their ranks with garden plants that pass our test of blending in well with their simple, graceful-looking character. We will seek to create a garden that is composed of plants that look as if they could be wild, most probably a mix of local natives, introduced species and a few simple and elegant hybrids. Being human, with an eye to artistry, we will seek to improve on nature, choosing the most attractive and arranging them in a subtle, understated way to create particular complements and pleasing contrasts of form and colour.

The repertoire of garden plants includes many that are practically identical to their wild ancestors, like lily of the valley (Convallaria majalis). Some are natives brought into gardens long ago, some exotics from compatible climates that have been introduced over the years. Old garden plants have sometimes moved on somewhat from their original identity, as gardeners selected forms that had particularly interesting features or colour variants – white bluebells or foxgloves, say – and some (like aquilegias) hybridized freely in gardens. However, the original species plants and their naturally occurring forms and hybrids generally possess the understated qualities we seek.

Plants we need to avoid are those where novelty-conscious plant breeders have been at work. Their priority is often to produce larger, longer-lasting blooms – often double – in previously unheard-of colours. Some plants, notably bearded irises, some of the day lilies, roses, peonies and florists' chrysanthemums, have been very intensively bred to produce a vast number of novel forms to appeal to fashion-conscious gardeners. The resulting artificial-looking cultivars look out of place among wildflowers or in any kind of setting that appear to look natural. However, alongside many of the 'improved' plants in these groups there remain some species and varieties – those of a more elegant mien or with relatively small flowers – that are compatible with a wilder style of gardening. Thus though many day lilies have become florid and graceless, individual cultivars such as Hemerocallis 'Golden Chimes' can be sufficiently fine to qualify; the species H. lilioasphodelus is altogether more delicate and has the bonus of scent. Similarly, we can ignore the hundreds of lush, large-flowered roses in cultivation, and instead focus on the dozens of less showy species with smaller flowers but often interesting leaves (R. glauca, for example), plus the bonus of hips in autumn.

Some people in the natural gardening movement argue that only locally native plants should be used because they are the ones most suited to the local environment and of most benefit to the ecosystem through their role in the food chain (page 26). They also fear that introducing exotics can result in troublesome 'escapes' of invasive species. While the first reason is valid, it overlooks the many non-native plants that come from similar climates and soils in other parts of the world and therefore will grow just as well. The second reason is certainly important and will matter to the keen wildlife gardener, but as we have seen there are some plants that birds and insects appreciate regardless of their place of origin.

The third reason – escapes – is perhaps the least supportable. Certainly a few plants introduced into cultivation have 'got out' and caused immense problems; Japanese knotweed (Fallopia japonica) is among the most infamous, spreading its herbicide-resistant shoots across Europe and North America. Yet compared to the total number of plants introduced into cultivation, the proportion that have become unwelcome guests is minute. Care should be exercised, though, with very vigorous species, or those that produce vast quantities of seedlings, in country areas. Particular care is necessary when planting alongside waterways; the worst troublemakers often either grow in water or spread along it – witness purple loosestrife (Lythrum salicaria), which has become a menace in many parts of North America. Good books and local garden advisory services and societies will often warn of potential problem species.

The effect may be very informal but the plant varieties here are mostly hybrids. The central peony and the surrounding aquilegias are all the result of many years' hybridizing, yet in the right context, framed by ferns and foxgloves, do not look artificial.

Planning for low maintenance

Low maintenance is an important consideration for people who lead busy lives, have a larger garden than they can cultivate themselves, or perhaps possess a second home with a garden.

We can define a low-maintenance garden as one which not only takes a relatively limited amount of time to look after, but also needs little irrigation, limited upkeep involving the frequent or repeated use of machinery, and an absolute minimum of chemicals to control weeds and pests or promote growth. Any planting is going to involve quite a lot of work at the beginning, perhaps for the first few years, while the new plants establish themselves, but after this it should be very much up to you to decide how much and how little time you want to devote to it.

What makes a garden naturally low-maintenance? The answer is partly in the selection of plants and partly in the way that they are put together. We saw in the Introduction (page 10) that plant communities are constantly changing, generally in the direction of reverting to woodland. The first stage in this process is the colonization of bare ground by the disturbance-tolerating plants, most of which we regard as weeds. The traditional garden with its expanses of bare earth between plants is a haven for these opportunistic plants. In other words, this kind of gardening *creates* work: every time one lot of weeds is hoed off, the ideal conditions are created for the germination of the next! Besides the perpetual task of controlling weeds, a fair proportion of the work that goes into the conventional garden is concerned with providing an environment for plants that would not live there naturally. The seasonal planting out of bedding plants is one obvious example, and improving drainage in order to grow plants intolerant of moisture another.

The style of gardening that we explore in this book reduces garden maintenance because it aims to create more or less self-maintaining plant communities, which keep the ground largely covered with a close blanket of vegetation. The plants chosen are ones that naturally grow well in the soil conditions and the prevailing climate of the garden, and thus do not need irrigation, protection from the cold, feeding or any of the other activities that result from trying to help plants to grow in places that they would not normally tolerate.

If the conditions described above are met and plants are chosen that are ecologically

This dry slope is clothed in a wide range of colourful, drought-resistant plants such as thymes, lavenders and bearded iris. Because these grow relatively slowly and are evergreen, maintenance is low.

suited to the garden, then an important part of the selection process is complete. But beyond this, some plants still need a lot more maintenance than others. As a general rule, plants that are closely related to their wild ancestors need relatively little care and attention. They do not grow so tall that they flop over in the slightest shower of rain, nor do they require feeding to give of their best, or painstaking pruning to coax them to flower. The same goes for simple hybrids between wild species, but the complex cultivars that are far removed from their wild ancestors are another story; mop-headed chrysanthemums and towering delphinium spires are notoriously labour-intensive, needing staking to prevent them from collapsing, and calling for feeding and often winter protection. Since they can only be propagated vegetatively, the gardening calendar has to include taking cuttings, dividing plants and so on to sustain a population of these demanding individuals. Simple natural beauty, on the other hand, is far more likely to mean simple natural care.

That care is further reduced if the customary maintenance regime of enriching the soil with quantities of manure and fertilizer traditionally used is discontinued. Certain methods of cultivation can create more work for the gardener. Original species, if richly fed, will grow much larger and laxer than they do in nature, and some may need staking to prevent frequent falling over. Hardy geraniums, for example, become such a mess after flowering in rich garden soil that they need

Compact plants need little maintenance to keep in shape. Here lavenders complement the pale yellow buttons of Santolina pinnata *subsp.* neapolitana *'Sulphurea' and the pale green heads of* Euphorbia characias *subsp.* wulfenii *in summer whilst the grasses will look attractive for months to come.*

to be cut back. With no extra feeding, these plants grow more compactly and more strongly. And when lax plants are grown intermingled, especially in the company of supporting grasses, they will lean on one other for support. Not only will the results be refreshingly different from the conventional garden, giving it a much more natural ambience, but the well-mingled plants will deny space to invasive and undesirable weedy species much more effectively than plants growing in discrete and separate clumps.

One aspect of maintenance that is crucial to the health of new perennial schemes is your mowing, strimming or dead-heading routine, and you do need to take this into account in your planning. The different kinds of planting require specific regimes. For instance, wildflower meadows and lawns are not cut until sometime in summer, when the flowering plants have set seed, and clippings are removed to avoid enriching the soil; you can, however, give prairie plants a trimming early in the year, because their peak of flowering comes in late summer.

Planning year-round interest

MOST SHADE-TOLERANT PLANTS flower in spring and most sun-loving meadow and border plants in summer, but by dovetailing perennials together with suitable bulbs and a framework of shrubs, trees and climbers, it is possible to create a succession of colour and interest all year round.

Winter and spring

Snowdrops (*Galanthus*) and winter aconites (*Eranthis*) are some of the first bulbs to flower in late winter, naturalizing easily in partly shaded sites to form extensive colonies. The mysteriously hued hellebores and several species of euphorbia are by nature shade-loving perennials, but in most latitudes they can be grown in full sun wherever the soil does not seriously dry out in summer. Their evergreen leaves, together with the occasional evergreen shrub, help to combat the emptiness of much of the garden in winter when most herbaceous plants have retreated below ground. Pulmonarias and dead-nettles (lamiums), too, begin to flower in late winter, but are also appreciated for their silver-splashed leaves, which bring summer colour to shaded areas.

As spring appears, a host of other bulbs begins to emerge and flower. Many daffodils, scillas, crocuses and tulips will thrive in light shade beneath trees (see page 52), beneath deciduous shrubs and around herbaceous perennials, providing colour at a time when the shrubs are still leafless and the perennials dormant. As the larger plants come into leaf, the bulbs die down.

A good many bulbs can be naturalized in grass that you leave uncut until the bulb

foliage has died down, to allow them to build up strength for the next season. Make sure you choose species that enjoy their permanent covering of turf, however; those that originate from regions with hot dry summers – the wonderful range of colourful wild tulips, for instance – need a good 'baking' to ripen them, which makes them unsuitable for growing beneath grass in most circumstances. A hot dry bank may be worth trying, or the thin vegetation of a dry-land planting on stony or sandy soil (see page 96) – a habitat where some wild tulips can even self-seed prolifically.

One of the most attractive springtime wildflower spectacles for the garden is sheets of pale yellow primroses (*Primula vulgaris*), violets, deep pink *Cyclamen repandum*, blue and white *Anemone blanda* cultivars and *A. nemorosa* growing in the thin grass beneath trees. All of these, the primroses especially, readily self-seed if mowing is delayed until midsummer.

Shady areas come into their own in spring (see page 48), with a wide variety of wildflowers, among them trilliums, blood-root (*Sanguinaria canadensis*) and Dutchman's breeches (*Dicentra*). Areas of border and meadow are best enlivened with bulbs, since comparatively few herbaceous plants flower this early. Exceptions are the yellow cowslips and oxlips (*Primula veris* and *P. elatior*), both of which can spread impressively if allowed to seed, and the violet or lavender pasque flowers (*Pulsatilla vulgaris* and others). Spring-flowering trees and shrubs also help to boost colour in the garden at this time.

Summer and autumn

The sunlight of summer offers optimum growing conditions, enabling many perennial plants to grow rapidly and vigorously, but the moisture factor has a strong controlling effect on the species that

will flourish and on the time of year the garden will look at its best.

Where the soil is on the moist side and reasonably fertile, strongly competitive plants will be at an advantage, making considerable lush growth in a surprisingly short time. Many of these flower only after midsummer, but in the meantime by early summer a garden on moist soil can have water-loving irises – yellow *Iris pseudacorus* and violet *I. versicolor* – and the bright pink flowers of ragged robin (*Lychnis flos-cuculi*), among others. As summer draws on, the combination of heat, sunlight and moisture encourages progressively taller vegetation, such as creamy meadowsweet (*Filipendula ulmaria*), best grown *en masse* as it does in nature, a superb foil for brighter coloured perennials. By late summer the host of plants in flower includes blue *Lobelia siphilitica* and scarlet cardinal flower (*Lobelia cardinalis*), pink and mauve bergamots (*Monarda*) and towering pale pink Joe Pye weed (*Eupatorium purpureum*).

In dry environments the summer sun brings heat and drought, often increasingly restricting growth as the year advances. Not surprisingly plants tend to flower early, with little growth later on. Early summer in a dry landscape garden can be supremely colourful. Bearded irises (*Iris germanica* hybrids) in myriad shades retain the tough drought-resistance of their wild ancestors to produce a sea of colour. Great mounds of red valerian (*Centranthus ruber*) foam out of the most unpromisingly stony sites, while flax (*Linum perenne*) spreads sheets of cooling blue among the brighter colours of other neighbouring plants.

By midsummer the intensity of flower colour is beginning to fade but the attractive foliage of drought-tolerant plants such as grey lavenders, artemisias and catmints

(*Nepeta*) still provides plenty of interest. Wild marjorams (*Origanum*) and knap-weeds (*Centaurea*) are among the perennials that can usually be relied upon to provide a splash of colour after midsummer. In addition there are the grasses that give such an extra dimension to dry habitats – the vast sprays of the seedheads of *Stipa gigantea*, steely blue *Helictotrichon* and *Elymus* species, and the incomparably soft plumes of pennisetums.

Shady environments may be cool and consequently moist through the summer, but lack of light under trees makes growth difficult for perennials. Lightly shaded areas can grow foxgloves (*Digitalis purpurea*) and astilbes; full shade has little to offer in the way of flowers, so make the most of the attractive foliage of many shade lovers – such as ferns, and the leaves of species such as epimediums and hostas that flowered earlier on in the year.

When the days start to get colder, flower numbers begin to wane. Autumn, however, brings many strong-growing members of the daisy family (Compositae) – rudbeckias,

The shapely seedheads of mullein, Scotch thistle, grasses and alliums, shown here in late summer, will continue to provide interest well into the winter.

asters, goldenrod (*Solidago*) – mostly in shades of yellow or blue and violet to complement the russet shades of autumnal trees. This is also when ornamental grasses are at their best, their seedheads continuing to look attractive in the winter months.

Colour and form

THE USE OF COLOUR AND FORM in gardens is an intensely personal matter. It is important to choose what you like, not what you feel you ought to like or what is currently fashionable (or what I suggest, for that matter!). Nevertheless, some basic rules seem to command general agreement. One is that soft pastel shades – pinks, blues and mauves – are easy to combine, are soothing and calming to look at and seem their best under grey skies and soft light. Another is that colours such as red, yellow and orange are 'hot', less restful and not so easy to blend.

The new perennial gardener looks, of course, to natural plant communities for inspiration. So what tips does nature offer? The good news is that a naturalistic approach to gardening does make colour planning easier. Whereas mixing highly bred, intensely coloured garden plants makes colour clashes all too frequent, using natural species – with more delicate flowers scattered more sparsely among foliage – results in fewer strong colours being concentrated together. The way that wildflowers grow, largely intermingled instead of in blocks of a single variety, means that the colours are seen in a

LEFT *Yellow mullein and lilies contrast well with blue-violet larkspur and dark red* Allium sphaerocephalon, *creating a harmonious picture of vibrant, complementary colours.*

RIGHT *An 'open border' planting style allows drifts of a particular colour combination to be repeated, but also to be interspersed with others which will flower later in the season.* Geranium × magnificum *flowers alongside* Alchemilla mollis *and a* Ranunculus acris *'Flore Pleno'.*

different way, as spots of colour on a green background rather than discrete areas. Pink with yellow, for example, is a combination that most of us agree does not work, and yet when seen together – as it often is in early summer in Central Europe, where yellow buttercups (*Ranunculus arvensis*) and bright pink ragged robin (*Lychnis flos-cuculi*) cover meadow after meadow – the effect is not so jarring.

Another reason that wildflower meadows nearly always look pleasing to the eye (despite being full of flowers that individually are often vividly coloured) is the role of white, cream and yellow-green flowers, many of them members of the cow parsley family (the Umbelliferae). These act as buffer colours, separating the stronger pinks, purples and yellows, and allowing them to blend together into one harmonious whole. On their own, these low-key plants can seem rather dull, but their place in the whole composition is quite crucial.

In the open borders favoured by new perennial gardeners, the flowers are less scattered and blended than in a wildflower meadow, and so colour co-ordination does play a more important role. There is no reason why a wide range of colours should not be brought together, but usually a limited palette will achieve a more powerful effect. Anyone who regularly visits gardens open to the public must remember seeing certain colour combinations that are instantly striking, often ones that we would not necessarily predict would work together. For example, a favourite of mine is the magenta *Geranium psilostemon* with pale blue or yellow green. Over the years I have seen this almost aggressive colour combined most successfully with *Geranium pratense* 'Mrs Kendall Clark' and *Veronica longifolia* (both pale blue) and *Euphorbia wallichii* (yellow-green).

Foliage qualities and plant form are as important as flower colour. Ornamental grasses, largely ignored in traditional borders, have a particularly important part to play. Some, such as the noble *Miscanthus* species, add majesty and bulk to a planting in late summer and autumn. The erect-growing *Calamagrostis* × *acutiflora* 'Karl Foerster' can be dotted around a planting to help to give it a vertical accent and unity. Others are primarily of value for the colour of their foliage. Many evergreen New Zealand sedges are particularly useful in this respect.

Plants with dramatic, architectural foliage, such as rhubarbs (*Rheum* species) and several 'thistles' (species of *Echinops*, *Onopordum* and *Cirsium*) have a particular role to play. They add an element of sculpture, and sometimes a touch of exoticism, too. Unless you are going all out to develop the sub-tropical look, though, it would be advisable to limit their numbers.

The orange of alstroemerias, day lilies (Hemerocallis) and heleniums consorts with the yellow of lilies, mulleins (left) and Achillea filipendulina, bringing the russet tones of autumn to midsummer. They are complemented by the silver stems of Artemisia ludoviciana, a plant useful from spring onwards for its attractive foliage. In late summer and autumn, goldenrods will be the main feature. Spring daffodils and, in early summer, low clump-forming geranium species could be intermingled with the later flowering perennials.

Designing plant groups

IN THE CONVENTIONAL BORDER, plants are generally grouped according to height, with the tallest against a boundary at the back and the shortest at the front, while in island beds the taller plants generally make a 'spine' in the centre. The open borders of the new perennial garden lack this emphasis on vertical structure and are more relaxed in style, with plants arranged in loose groups of varying sizes scattered across the planted area rather than in clearly delimited, discrete clumps. This scattering, and the consequent blending of varieties, gives these plantings a sense of both unity and naturalness. In a wild meadow, certain species naturally rise above others. In a garden planting we want to copy this effect, but we also need to arrange plants so that they are displayed to maximum effect at the time they look their best.

A crucial factor is to consider the impact of each plant and whether it looks best planted singly, in small groups or larger masses. 'Plant sociability' is the measure of the size of group into which it is appropriate to put plants. Different varieties can be classed according to their sociability on a I to V scale. Plants which are by nature

Bearded irises, along with many of the low-growing rockery-type plants featured here, such as sedums and thymes, need to be grown in clumps to have much impact in the garden. All Group IV and V plants, they have 'high sociability'. Others, like valerian (seen here in both its red and white forms), can be a bit overwhelming as well as dull when not in flower. It is thus a good idea to allow this Group II plant to make only small drifts or scattered incidents – its sociability is lower.

statuesque, looking best in splendid isolation from their fellows, can be classed as I, those that look best either on their own or in small, rather scattered clusters as II. Examples might be the erect-growing grass *Calamagrostis × acutiflora* 'Karl Foerster' or the large eupatorium species. Those that leave large bare gaps after flowering (such as *Papaver orientale*) or take up a lot of space (such as peonies) are also regarded as I or II plants. Group III plants are those that look or work best in larger clumps – many perennials which produce a single flower spike (such as foxgloves or *Dictamnus albus*). Groups IV and V are mostly ground-cover and other low-growing plants. Except in tiny gardens, IV plants, like epimediums, are only effective when grouped; V plants, like prostrate thymes are are insignificant unless grown in large patches. Particularly striking effects can be had by combining I and II plants with IV and V ones, so that small scattered groups of plants of fine form (ferns and bamboos, for example) rise out of low, carpeting ones such as ivy or periwinkle.

The relative tightness or looseness of groups is related to the formality of the planting. Open borders generally use quite clearly distinct groupings of plants, much like conventional 'ribbon' borders, whereas in the meadow or wildflower garden, loose groupings are more appropriate, with the boundaries of each group blurring into the next and some plants being scattered almost randomly across the planting.

Whilst shade-loving plants can be mingled attractively, their compact growth makes them naturally suited for growing in distinct clumps. Epimediums, hostas, vincas and Tellima grandiflora, *with its spires of bell-shaped flowers, can all be regarded as sociability group III and IV plants, and planting them together in groups shows off their form and foliage to best advantage.*

As well as thinking about what size of group plants look best in, you also need to take into account the season at which they flower and what those groups will look like once the plants have finished flowering. In spring there is little to be seen; most perennials are only just coming around from dormancy, so bulbs and early perennials can be scattered widely. Many of the shade-tolerant early plants such as pulmonarias and primulas will benefit from later shading by taller perennials and shrubs. By the earlier part of the summer perennials such as geraniums will be flowering, generally at heights of 60 cm / 24 in or less. They too can be scattered through a planting as there will be little – other than perhaps the occasional shrub – to hide them from view. Only those that leave tidy clumps after flowering should be placed at the front, though; geums, for example, always look tidy, whereas many

geraniums do not and are therefore better placed farther back. Later-flowering perennials tend to be tall, sometimes very tall. The very tallest ones can, of course, be at the back, as they would be when planted conventionally, although the majestic habit of many is best appreciated if they are planted nearer the front. Those of medium height are best nearer the middle or the front, so that they will not be hidden by – and indeed will help to obscure – the dying remains of earlier-flowering perennials.

When planning a planting the structural plants – shrubs and architectural (sociability I) perennials – should be marked out first, followed by the theme perennials, and then the rest. It is often useful to lay out the low-growing (sociability IV and V varieties) after the taller plants. Spring-flowering bulbs can usually be left until last, to fill in spaces that will be bare early in the year.

This planting, on rather dry soil, is best in early summer, when yellow achilleas and purple Salvia nemorosa *hybrids dominate. They are the 'theme plants' for this season, and in fact for the planting as a whole. Later on in the year other perennials and biennials, interplanted between those that are currently flowering, will provide some interest, especially the majestic* Salvia sclarea *var.* turkestanica, *now only visible as large leaves.*

Totally invisible as yet are the asters, varieties of the relatively drought-tolerant A. amellus, *which will lie low until their late-summer/autumn flowering time nears. Because they remain small and neat for most of the season, they are useful for putting in at the front of a planting.*

The scattered pink lychnis are the result of self-sowing. A few plants in the initial scheme can usually be guaranteed to produce many more seedlings, replacing the somewhat short-lived originals. If they become a nuisance, some 'creative weeding' may be necessary.

Salvias and achilleas are sociability group II and III plants, looking their best in small to medium sized clumps (three to five plants each). The later-flowering asters and sedums can be treated similarly. The grasses here, though, have more architectural qualities and are best appreciated grown singularly or in small loose groupings of three; they are group I or II plants.

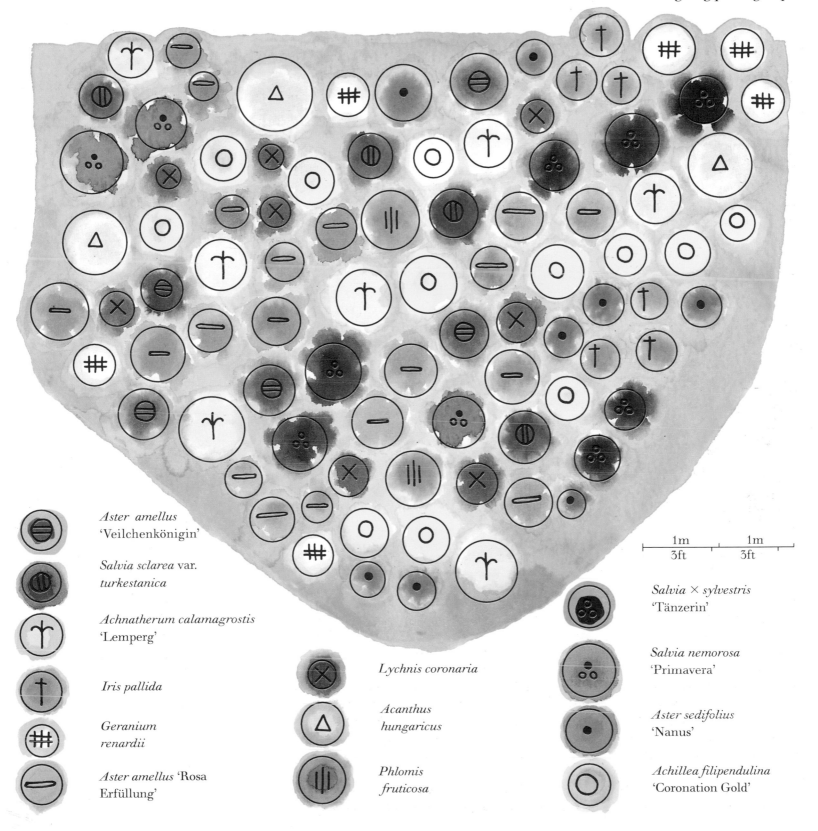

Aster amellus 'Veilchenkönigin'

Salvia sclarea var. turkestanica

Achnatherum calamagrostis 'Lemperg'

Iris pallida

Geranium renardii

Aster amellus 'Rosa Erfüllung'

Lychnis coronaria

Acanthus hungaricus

Phlomis fruticosa

1m 1m
3ft 3ft

Salvia × sylvestris 'Tänzerin'

Salvia nemorosa 'Primavera'

Aster sedifolius 'Nanus'

Achillea filipendulina 'Coronation Gold'

Establishing successful plantings

Successful plantings are those composed of plants chosen for their ability to grow well in their new home in a site that has been well prepared. The most important part of this preparation is the removal of perennial weed roots, which can be done by a variety of means, chemical and physical. The kind of plantings outlined in this book will prevent weed infiltration reasonably well once they have become established, but they must be given a chance to mature first. Weed clearance and other aspects of site preparation are dealt with in detail on pages 114-5.

The main way in which plants prevent weeds from growing is by covering the ground with growth which inhibits the survival of weed seedlings. Nevertheless, during winter and during the establishment phase of a planting, weed seeds may germinate in spaces between dormant perennials or before the perennials have started to grow and spread, a problem we look at on page 128. In plantings which involve a number of short-lived perennials – those that need to keep on reproducing themselves by seed to maintain themselves in the border – a certain amount of bare ground will be necessary for the self-seeding to take place, which unfortunately can also act as a seed bed for weeds. Such areas will thus need more intensive maintenance than if the whole area was covered with longer-lived perennials.

The problem with weed growth in the establishment phase can be reduced by several means, such as mulching with various natural or synthetic materials and also by planting more densely than usual –

When plants intermingle like these aquilegias, euphorbias, Welsh poppies (Meconopsis cambrica) *and male ferns* (Dryopteris filix-mas), *they all need to be of a similar level of competitiveness, so that some do not overpower others.*

at about twice the normal rate — so that growth covers the ground more quickly. This will also have the advantage of making the planting look established within a year. However, it has the disadvantage that close planting increases competition between plants, shortening the life of many, and giving opportunities to the more aggressive to take over. Thinning out and replanting would thus be needed after only three years.

Fertile soils encourage vigorous growth, so choose the more competitive plants. The ox-eye daisies and hawkweed (Pilosella aurantiaca) *flowering here with lady's mantle might be too rampant for a tidy border but flourish in a wilder garden.*

Since herbaceous perennial plantings mature so quickly anyway — three years is usually enough to make them look settled — such dense planting does seem unnecessary in most circumstances. If large gaps between plants for the first two years seem especially undesirable, you could consider temporary sowings of lower-growing annuals such as nigella, linum and calendula to fill the spaces. They will help to reduce weed competition, although if planted too densely and too close to young perennials they could become weeds in their own right!

A good planting distance for most perennials is around five or six plants per square metre or square yard, three to four plants for larger or bushy varieties, and 10 to 12 for

small, low-growing plants. As a general rule the spread given in most gardening books can be used as a rough guide, but you can usually reduce the distance between the plants to a little under the figure given.

In certain circumstances there may be tenacious weeds that are simply impossible to get rid of; ground elder and horsetail are two examples. In such cases the best thing is to isolate them from the rest of the garden with an area of regularly mown grass or plant around them with strong-growing competitive perennials which will prevent them from establishing dominance. Geraniums, hellebores, lamiums and astrantia are examples that live with ground elder in nature.

Shade plantings

Lack of light need not mean dark and gloom. Plants from naturally shady woodland habitats can be used to create an environment that is interesting for a long season, and the fact that many are evergreen and have attractive foliage is to their advantage.

Shade varies greatly, from the deep, dry shade beneath conifers to the dappled shade of a woodland edge, or from the sunless side of a building to a site where there is sun for half the day. Shade varies with the seasons, too, and the greater light beneath leafless winter trees enables many woodlanders to flower gratifyingly early. In addition, the moisture and nutrient content of the soil affects how plants react to shade, with high levels of both tending to counteract the lack of light. Understanding these variations is the key to successful shade planting.

Because they are natural woodlanders, foxgloves (Digitalis purpurea) and columbines (Aquilegia hybrids) flourish in partial shade but are adaptable enough to cope with more open sites. They spread by self-sowing on many soils. Plant different colour forms to bring an element of serendipity to future seedlings.

Shade means shortage of light, one of the most essential requirements for healthy growth for a plant. It is not therefore surprising that many plants do not grow well if they find themselves in shade.

A walk in natural woodland from shade underneath trees into the light reveals quite dramatic changes in vegetation, changes which have importance for the gardener. In the darkest shade, there may only be a few sparse growths of very tolerant species such as ivy (an evergreen) or a few spring bulbs. In less dense shade there is frequently a profusion of species. Their growth is often thoroughly intertwined, but it is still quite sparse, with many gaps between the plants, where the dead leaves of last autumn remain on the bare soil. As light increases, so does the density and height of the vegetation. In half shade there will be fewer of the low, clump-forming plants like hellebores and epimediums that are typical of full shade, and more of the taller plants like foxgloves (*Digitalis*) and campanulas whose upright habit is more characteristic of open habitats. Growth will be denser, as competition is fiercer, which is a reminder to the gardener to ensure that such areas in the garden are planted with complete ground

TOP LEFT *Shade-tolerant species tend to form distinct clumps. This path winds past ground-covering patches of hostas, ferns, London pride* (Saxifraga × urbium), *euphorbia and dicentra on the left. White-flowered corydalis makes a mound of fine foliage in the right foreground.*

LEFT *Ferns like the* Adiantum pedatum *scattered through this planting are a must in damp, shady conditions. They contrast well with larger leaves such as the heart shapes of epimediums. White touches in the flowers of corydalis, tiarella and a Solomon's seal with outlined leaves lighten the gloom.*

cover, otherwise weeds will gain a foothold.

For our purposes 'full shade' (see page 48) means that an area receives less than two hours of direct sun a day. 'Light shade' (see page 50) is where sunlight reaches for between two hours and half a day, or where broken light comes through the leaf canopy. 'Problem shade' (see page 52) is where lack of sunlight is compounded by drought and infertility or is caused by the proximity of buildings. 'Transitional shade' takes its cue from the natural woodland edge (see page 54) where shade conditions can fluctuate over time.

Looking at natural plant communities in full shade, one of the first things you notice is that the grassy matrix so basic to plant communities in sunlight is absent. The majority of grasses, along with other highly competitive plants (including most weeds), do not grow well in shade, leaving the field open to more stress-tolerant species. Many of these make desirable garden plants.

As well as poor light, there is often a distinct lack of nutrients under trees, and sometimes lack of moisture too, the trees monopolizing both. However, humidity is higher, which means that less water is lost by evaporation from the soil and transpiration by ground-level plants. In addition, on many soils a layer of humus builds up from the autumn leaf-fall, and this highly moisture-retentive medium offers a cool and moist root-run that suits many plants. Leaf-fall itself can be a problem, annually smothering ground-level vegetation with a soggy blanket of dead leaves. Grasses are particularly badly affected by this.

To cope with the lack of such an essential element as light, woodland plants have adopted a number of survival strategies, some of which have a positive advantage for the gardener. One is having evergreen leaves that can take advantage of light all through the year, including the winter, when the

trees are leafless; hellebores and deadnettles (lamiums) are good examples. The foliage of many of these plants is very attractive, which is useful given that the season of flower in shade can be restricted.

Another survival strategy is to flower and grow as much as possible early in the year, before the trees come into leaf. So it is not surprising that shady habitats are particularly colourful in spring, with violets, wood anemones and primroses, or bulbs like snowdrops (*Galanthus*) and scillas. Indeed many early flowering woodland plants have bulbs or tubers which store nutrients for rapid growth early in the year.

While lack of light makes growth difficult in shade, the presence of a fertile soil or a relatively high moisture content does much to counteract this disadvantage. Moist shade, indeed, can be a singularly rewarding environment in which to garden. Ferns will love it, and the diversity and almost universal elegance of their form can be an endless source of fascination. Moist shade that is not too dense will also support plants such as astilbes – lush growers with feathery flower heads in shades of red, pink and white, their relatives the majestic aruncus, several large daisy-family plants such as ligularias, and the Candelabra primulas such as *P. japonica* and *P. prolifera* (formerly *P. helodoxa*), whose flowers offer a bewildering range of colour. Such plants will provide a much longer season of colour than can be hoped for in less moist shade.

Anemone blanda, *available in many colour forms, is one of the best small spring flowers to establish in the shade around the base of trees in light grass. Eventually it will self-seed, producing progeny in yet more shades. It needs moist conditions and moderate sunlight early in the year.*

Full shade

Spring is the time when shady gardens come into their own. Violets, primroses, oxlips (*Primula elatior*), anemones and *Cyclamen repandum* can carpet the ground with their flowers. Many of the early-flowering woodland plants that have bulbs or tubers thrive not only in the bare ground beneath trees but also in the lighter shade where grass will grow, albeit weakly. It is thus possible to grow them in thin grass, so long as the blades of the mower are set reasonably high, and cutting delayed until after their seeds have set.

Some shade-lovers have attractively coloured foliage, many of the pulmonarias being among the most rewarding. Even after their long flowering season, from late winter to almost the end of spring, the foliage of those varieties with silver-speckled leaves continues to give pleasure.

Later in spring the perennials that flower tend to be larger. They include the often strangely shaped and coloured trilliums, the easy and robust blue periwinkles (*Vinca* species), the arching stems of Solomon's seals (*Polygonatum*) and the tighter clumps of false Solomon's seal (*Smilacina*). As the

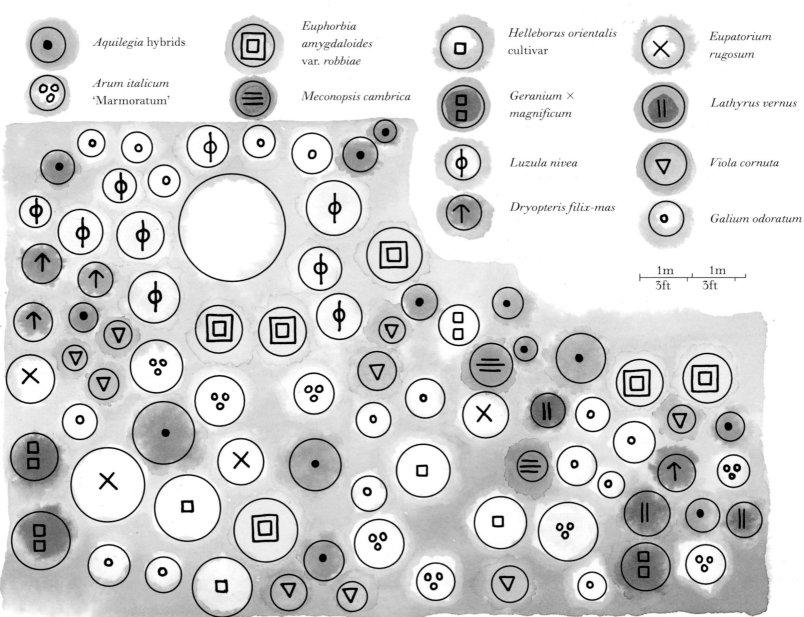

Aquilegia hybrids

Arum italicum 'Marmoratum'

Euphorbia amygdaloides var. *robbiae*

Meconopsis cambrica

Helleborus orientalis cultivar

Geranium × *magnificum*

Luzula nivea

Dryopteris filix-mas

Eupatorium rugosum

Lathyrus vernus

Viola cornuta

Galium odoratum

1m   1m
3ft   3ft

leaves on the trees mature, the scope for growth is increasingly limited, and the quantity of flower decreases.

The main joy for the months of summer is the often attractive foliage of shade-loving plants; the rather majestic lobed leaves of bloodroot (*Sanguinaria canadensis*), for example, or the robust rich green clumps of *Smilacina racemosa* leaves and, of course, of various fern fronds. Ferns are the supreme adornment to the woodland or shaded garden, at least if the soil is tolerably moist. There is a huge range and variety in fern foliage, from the completely undivided strap-like *Asplenium scolopendrium* to the intricate and seemingly endless subdivision of the fronds of *Polystichum setiferum*. Size and habit varies, too; most of the *Dryopteris* clan form substantial plants whose fronds arch outwards, whereas the polystichums are lower and squatter. There are also ferns (such as thelypteris) which run sideways to form extensive ground cover.

Among the few plants that flower in summer, the perennial honesty (*Lunaria rediviva*) is excellent, its lavender flowers filling the evening air with fragrance in early summer. Like the foxgloves, this plant is a short-lived disturbance tolerator, but freely produces large quantities of rapidly germinating seed. Such plants benefit from a little forking over of areas of bare soil in their vicinity every year, to enable the seeds to be given a chance to grow.

Late summer sees the flowering of the highly distinctive cimicifugas with tall, narrow spikes of white or cream flowers. They do not need moisture, but hate drying

The variety of plant interest possible in a heavily shaded site is well demonstrated here. The white-veined foliage of Arum italicum *'Marmoratum' is surrounded by yellow euphorbias, blue aquilegias and evergreen hellebore leaves.*

out or getting too hot and also dislike too much competition. It is worth catering to their needs as they are magnificent and there may be little other colour at this time.

Perhaps the most reliable plants for this time of year in shade are the Japanese anemones (*Anemone × hybrida*). These hybrids derived from *A. hupehensis* and *A. tomentosa* thrive in shade that is not too deep on reasonably moist soils, building up over the years – after a slow start – into substantial clumps that give a long season of large white or pink flowers.

Also colourful late in the year are the berries of species of baneberry (*Actaea*), especially *A. rubra*, which is red and *A. alba*, white. Both thrive in similar conditions to cimicifugas.

Being relatively uncompetitive and slow-growing plants, shade-lovers can usually be mixed to grow happily together for many years. Even those that spread, such as *Anemone nemorosa* or the woodruff *Galium odoratum*, do not smother their neighbours. The main work involved in maintenance is the removal of leaves in autumn where they cover evergreen species. The leaves should be composted or shredded and then applied as a mulch around the plants. Occasional tree seedlings may also have to be removed. Unfortunately for the gardener, the slow-growing nature of many shade-lovers, including many of the most delightful, means that they are very slow to propagate and to become established. Some, trilliums and orchids especially, are threatened with extinction because of wild collection, which means that it is important to check the provenance of these plants from anyone offering them for sale.

Problem shade

Sʜᴀᴅʏ ᴄᴏɴᴅɪᴛɪᴏɴs in which the soil is reasonably fertile and moist offer only one major stress to plants: lack of light. Where this is compounded by drought and infertility – often caused by tree roots near to the surface – these three causes of stress severely limit the number of plants that will grow. Dry shade has the terrible reputation among gardeners for being the most difficult of all places to make flourish. But there are a number of plants of varying habit that can make dry shade more interesting. None of them – it has to be said – particularly relishes growing in these conditions; it is just that they cope some-what better than any others! The rather magnificent sedge *Carex pendula* will lift the tone of such a spot, along with the male fern (*Dryopteris filix-mas*) and the impressive dark clump of foliage formed by *Helleborus foetidus*. A number of ground covers will cope: the vincas will send out sprawling branches that will gradually take root; *Tellima grandiflora* can be planted in clumps and may well self-seed, while *Euphorbia amygdaloides* var. *robbiae* will spread adventurously almost anywhere.

For flowers, there are several hardy geraniums to choose from. *Geranium macrorrhizum*, which in nature grows on dry hillsides, thrives in shade to flower in various shades of pink in early summer; the blue-purple *G. himalayense* blooms later in the summer. *Campanula latifolia* seems to do well enough so long as it does not get too dry, and foxgloves (*Digitalis purpurea*) are worth trying, too.

The greatest delight of dry shade – for a small-scale, carpeting effect – is *Cyclamen hederifolium*, which begins to flower in late summer, sending up leaves somewhat later to spread themselves over the ground and

take maximum advantage of the leafless trees above through the winter. This is one of those plants that seems to thrive around the base of tree trunks. Another, for early spring, is the winter aconite (*Eranthis hyemalis*), which once established will self-seed to spread its yellow flowers widely.

Few ferns will thrive in dry soil. Among those that do – beside the male fern – are many polystichums, like the usefully evergreen *P. acrostichoides*.

Deep shade is another problem, where overhead branches make it positively dark at ground level. Deep shade nearly always seems to be aggravated by the additional problems of drought and infertility, making it an even worse prospect. In the relatively infrequent situation where there is a moist soil in deep shade, a good number of ferns will thrive, but elsewhere only ivies and a few other redoubtable plants are capable of surviving at all.

Different kinds of tree cast different kinds of shade. Beech is notorious for the heavy shade of its leaf canopy, but a beechwood in spring is light enough for early-flowering bulbs and perennials such as *Galium*

Damp shade offers ideal growing conditions for lush, vigorous plants; most of these leafy clumps will bear flowers in late summer. Now, in spring, colour is provided by pink dodecatheon, blue ajuga and a sprinkling of bright little viola faces.

odoratum and *Anemone nemorosa*. The problem of deep shade is often exacerbated by the effects of heavy leaf-fall, especially when those leaves take a long time to decay. Some trees have leaves which break down relatively quickly – oaks (*Quercus*), for ex-ample – whereas others take much longer, which has a considerably inhibiting effect on vegetation; maples (*Acer*) are bad in this respect, so is beech (*Fagus*), and worst of all are horse chestnuts and buckeyes (*Aesculus*). Collecting up leaves and shredding or composting them into leaf-mould will help to make the environment a more friendly one for plants.

The permanent shade beneath conifers is, of course, one that winter-growing plants cannot cope with, and consequently this is an environment that is almost impossible. One perennial that will grow – at least if the

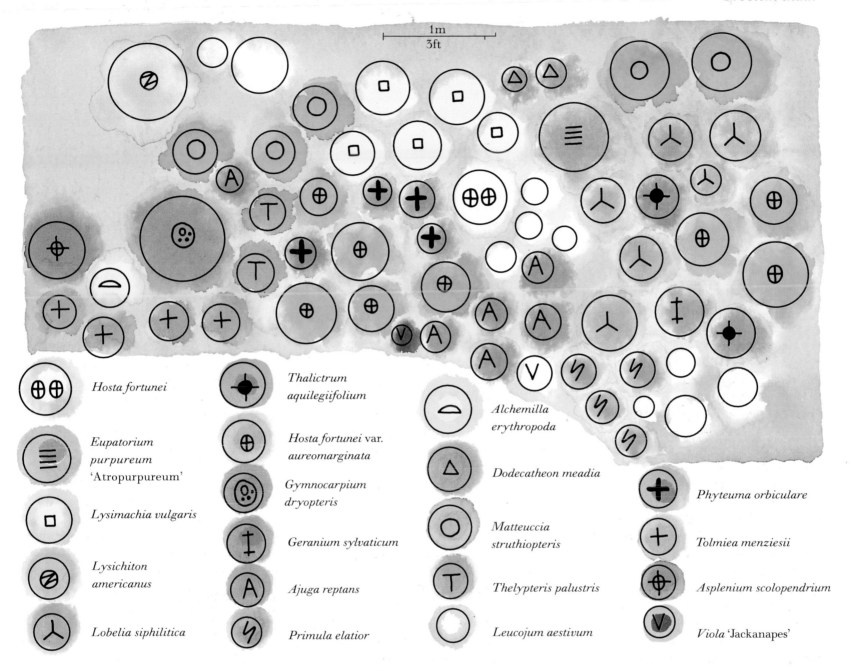

1m
3ft

Hosta fortunei	Thalictrum aquilegiifolium	Alchemilla erythropoda
Eupatorium purpureum 'Atropurpureum'	Hosta fortunei var. aureomarginata	Dodecatheon meadia
Lysimachia vulgaris	Gymnocarpium dryopteris	Matteuccia struthiopteris
Lysichiton americanus	Geranium sylvaticum	Thelypteris palustris
Lobelia siphilitica	Ajuga reptans	Leucojum aestivum
	Primula elatior	

Phyteuma orbiculare

Tolmiea menziesii

Asplenium scolopendrium

Viola 'Jackanapes'

ground is not too dry – is the white butter-bur (*Petasites albus*), which has large heart-shaped leaves and very early white flowers.

Not all shade is produced by trees, of course. Unlike the shade that trees produce, the shade cast by buildings offers no compensating advantages such as a reduction in wind velocity (which helps to reduce moisture loss) or a humus-rich soil. So often the soil around buildings is impoverished by its proximity to the foundations and suffers a lack of water caused by overhanging eaves. Building a raised bed to hold more and better-quality soil may be an artificial answer to an artificial problem, and this may enable you to grow a wide range of woodlanders, including trilliums. The addition of copious quantities of compost and other humus-rich organic matter may help overcome the problems of poor soil; planting shrubs or erecting wind-filtering fencing may help to reduce draughts; otherwise, your plant selection must be limited to those species that tolerate dry shade.

Light shade

THE EXTRA LIGHT in areas which are in sun for a few hours a day or where dappled sunlight falls in patches beneath trees – together with the generally higher nutrient level of the soil – is an easier environment for plants than full shade. Many sun-loving plants, especially grasses, still find survival a struggle and so plant communities are often relatively open and uncompetitive. This makes weed competition somewhat greater than in full shade.

Light shade is ideal for spring bulbs such as crocuses, daffodils and narcissi, squills (*Scilla* species) and chionodoxas, which are easily naturalized alongside shade-lovers, for example wood anemones and primroses. Late winter and spring also see hellebores in flower and the green-flowered, purple-leaved wood spurge

(*Euphorbia amygdaloides*), both of which are not only attractive evergreens, helping suppress weed infiltration, but also tolerate somewhat dry summer conditions.

Fertile soils with an average moisture content provide growing conditions in which relatively competitive plants thrive. Plantings in such areas must therefore have a mix of fairly vigorous species. Deadnettles flower earlier in the season, and their evergreen white-splashed leaves contribute year-round interest. Hardy geraniums, lady's mantle (*Alchemilla mollis*), comfrey (*Symphytum* species) and columbine (*Aquilegia vulgaris*) will mesh together to form a solid weed-proof mat of vegetation. These plants are at their best in early summer, with their pinks, blues and violets complemented by the cool yellow-green of the lady's mantle. By midsummer, most will have finished flowering, although many of the pink hardy geraniums will

flower off and on until the autumn. Hemerocallis are vigorous enough to co-exist with these plants, and flower in a variety of yellows, oranges and browns.

On moist soils astilbes and aruncus will thrive, and on distinctly soggy acid soils, Candelabra primulas such as *Primula japonica* and *P. pulverulenta* can be encouraged to create carpets of early to midsummer colour. Less moist acid soils are ideal for the supremely colourful creeping phloxes such as *P. stolonifera*, which has pink, blue and white varieties.

Less fertile or drier soils do not support strong-growers like geraniums so well, and it is best to combine these with more stress-tolerant species such as bluebells (*Hyacinthoides non-scripta*). These grow easily from seed, though like many bulbs will take several years to flower and more still to make spring carpets of blue. On moister soils bluebells are best grown in a plant community of slightly more vigorous species – a wonderful blue, pink and white mix combines them with red campion (*Silene dioica*), greater stitchwort (*Stellaria holostea*) and cow parsley (*Anthriscus sylvestris*).

On relatively infertile soils foxgloves (*Digitalis purpurea*) grow well, setting prodigious quantities of easily germinating seed. In nature their colonies grow and die out rapidly; in the garden you can encourage them to persist by a certain amount of annual soil disturbance to discourage the growth of rival plants that might crowd out the new seedlings.

Relatively few late summer or autumn flowers enjoy light shade. The white wood aster (*Aster divaricatus*) is a little subtle on its own, but when grown *en masse* creates a delightful haze of white daisies. For more dramatic clouds of white flowers, the white snakeroot (*Eupatorium rugosum*) stands out well against a dark background.

LEFT *Here springing up through last year's autumn leaves,* Cyclamen coum *and snowdrops are among the earliest flowers of the year. Flowering before the leaf canopy forms, they will naturalize in shade, for example at the base of tree trunks, where grass growth is weak.*

ABOVE *Ground hugging phloxes, such as this lavender* Phlox divaricata, *are some of the most colourful flowers for light shade in spring. Honesty* (Lunaria annua) *is a biennial which seeds itself among the phloxes. The arching white Solomon's seal* (Polygonatum multiflorum) *also thrives in deeper shade.*

Shrubs and hedges

IF YOU HAVE A TRANSITION zone between shade and sunlight in the garden, you can add to its attractiveness and interest by copying what nature does – planting shrubs and climbers and establishing perennials that are appropriate to the mosaic of different and changing light intensities.

The edge of natural woodland or forest is usually marked by a thick growth of shrubs and herbaceous plants that can make the most of the increased light. Climbers and scramblers are common, too, many with their roots and lower parts in shade and their upper, flowering parts in the sun. Such an environment is not only rich in wildflowers but in insects and birds too, because there is so much variation in light intensity within a small space – deep shade tolerated by woodlanders only a few paces from an almost completely open habitat. However, even when seemingly wild, these transition zones are often created or maintained by human intervention, either because trees have been felled, thus opening up an area to light, or because an area of disused open land is being taken over by scrub and young trees. As trees grow they reduce the light and thus shift the balance in favour of shade-tolerant plants; when they are cleared, light-lovers come to the fore. In addition, there are various kinds of managed environment that favour a rich mix of wild plants and animals – hedgerows are one, coppiced woodland another.

If you need to create a hedge, take the opportunity to plant it up with a variety of shrubs and climbers, with wildflowers along the base. Choosing appropriate shrubs for the new perennial garden is obviously important. Their size and permanence has a major impact on the overall feel of a plot. Many of the wide range of shrubs offered by garden centres are hybrids or cultivars, with the double flowers or variegated foliage which seem inappropriate in a more naturalistic garden. Unlike herbaceous perennials, which can be found in greatest variety on more alkaline soils, shrub species are to be had in their greatest abundance on relatively infertile acid ones. Wildly exuberant rhododendron species, mountain laurel (*Kalmia latifolia*), and flowering dogwoods (such as *Cornus florida*), for example, all flourish on such soils. On alkaline ones wild roses are among the most colourful, although many have a habit that is more scrambler or climber than shrub. Hollies (*Ilex*) also thrive on alkaline soils, as do euonymus, many with attractive fruit and brilliant autumn colour, and viburnums, although these usually have the added attraction of conspicuous flowers as well.

Shrubs do take much longer than perennials to reach their mature sizes, and there is consequently a great temptation to plant too many too closely. Unless they are thinned out at some stage, the result can be an impenetrable thicket in later years. Spaces between growing shrubs can always be filled with perennials, leaving them to be shaded out as the shrubs grow.

Traditional country hedges are an immensely rich habitat for wildlife, offering

LEFT *A fairly recent hedgerow planting is dominated by colourful short-lived perennials such as foxgloves, sweet rocket or dame's violet, red campion and a budding teasel. All will self-seed for several years but may well be replaced by others later.*

everything from full sun to full shade within a short distance. They have great potential in the garden, as a wide variety of shrubs can be blended together – not just traditional hedging shrubs like hawthorn (*Crataegus monogyna*), but also more ornamental species like the evergreen and winter-flowering *Viburnum tinus* or amelanchiers, that are so useful for their spring flowers, autumn colour and berries (which birds love).

Once the shrubs have been given two years to establish, the base of the hedge can be planted up with wildflowers and grasses, forming a band on each side which can be from only 30 cm/12 in to more than a metre/40 in wide. Sun-lovers can go on the brighter side, shade-tolerant species on the

other. Climbers such as wild roses, honey-suckles (*Lonicera* species) and clematis will help to strengthen the hedge.

Coppicing is a traditional means of woodland management that favours a rich and varied wildflower flora, and one that offers novel and interesting possibilities for the garden, too. The basic principle is that trees are cut to ground level every five to ten years, so that they send up a clump of new shoots (which in the past would have been used for a variety of purposes such as fencing). The ground underneath experiences a cyclical pattern of light and shade over the years, a constantly changing environment that suits the lifestyle of many short-lived woodland-edge plants such as foxgloves and campions (*Silene*).

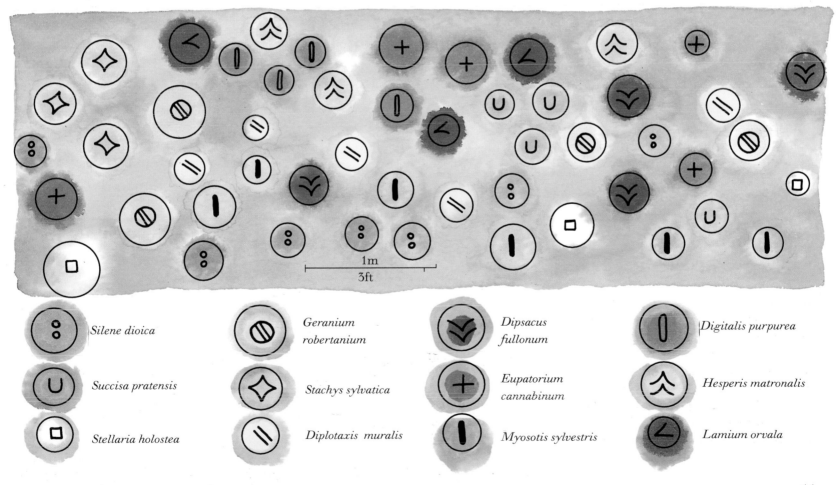

1m
3ft

Silene dioica	Silene dioica
Succisa pratensis	Succisa pratensis
Stellaria holostea	Stellaria holostea
Geranium robertanium	Geranium robertanium
Stachys sylvatica	Stachys sylvatica
Diplotaxis muralis	Diplotaxis muralis
Dipsacus fullonum	Dipsacus fullonum
Eupatorium cannabinum	Eupatorium cannabinum
Myosotis sylvestris	Myosotis sylvestris
Digitalis purpurea	Digitalis purpurea
Hesperis matronalis	Hesperis matronalis
Lamium orvala	Lamium orvala

Plantings in full sun

MOST OF US WHO LIVE IN TEMPERATE LATITUDES prefer our gardens to be in the sun. Although we may sometimes seek respite in the shade, we ideally want gardens that look resplendent on warm summer days, with the sun's rays beaming upon myriad flowers. Sun gives the plant world a chance to shine, particularly to treat us to its most radiant colours. Sun-loving herbaceous perennials cover the entire spectrum, offering the gardener an almost limitless palette to experiment with. These plants can be grown in a wide variety of different settings, from the majestic prairie to a tiny wildflower lawn.

Wildflower meadows are the inspiration for this romantic drift of subtle colour harmonies. In early summer different forms of self-seeding Aquilegia *hybrids mingle with* peonies, *the spherical flower heads of* Allium hollandicum *and the poppy* Papaver orientale. *Farther back, the cranesbill* Geranium pyrenaicum *forms a mauve-pink haze.*

Lawns and borders, the component parts of the conventional garden, are very much creatures of open sunny conditions. So are the open borders and meadows of more naturally inspired gardens. Full sun provides ideal conditions for the majority of plants that are grown in our gardens. In some places a sunny aspect may, of course, become almost too much of a good thing, with drought as a consequence, but even this extreme does not rule out the possibility of a beautiful garden.

In nature the open habitats that we see are overwhelmingly dominated by grasses. This is not generally the natural climax vegetation (see page 10); grassland in the form of meadow or pasture is usually prevented from being overtaken by scrub and trees only by the process of human maintenance. Truly natural grasslands are kept in being (or were kept – many have now been destroyed by agriculture) by climatic conditions that favour frequent fires, or by insufficient rainfall for tree growth. Grasses have an amazing ability to colonize bare ground and to dominate the

ABOVE *Although relatively infertile, a bank of sandy spoil from a pond excavation is fine for meadow wildflowers like ox-eye daisies and knapweed. Larger, more vigorous garden perennials grow in a conventional border beyond a mown grass strip.*

plant communities of sites open to the sun. Indeed, such is this colonizing ability that parts of the garden that we choose to keep grass-free (borders, for example) will inevitably demand more maintenance than those areas where we choose to compromise with this adventurous, physiologically efficient and tenacious group of plants. The latter areas include wildflower lawns, meadows and prairies. In the cultivation of these types of planting, flowering plants are given the same programme of maintenance as the matrix of grasses. Such garden habitats are maintained by mowing, which in itself helps to restrict the growth of the more vigorous grasses and wildflowers.

Shade, as we have seen, does not favour grasses. Neither do very infertile soils, which is why acidic soils tend to be covered with

dwarf shrubs such as heathers, and why dwarf shrubs and succulents come to the fore in very dry semi-desert habitats. High mountain environments, where the growing season is short and soil next to non-existent, also do not favour grasses. Elsewhere, they dominate, their exceptionally efficient metabolism enabling them to take maximum advantage of all available light, water and nutrients. Other plants,

ABOVE *A sowing of blue and white forms of meadow cranesbill* (Geranium pratense) *enlivens a bank of excavated subsoil. Happy in dry or damp soils, this is an adaptable wildflower for garden use.*

LEFT *Cornflowers and poppies were once regarded as weeds because they competed with field crops, but are now welcomed as garden flowers. As annuals they are not a permanent feature; sow them to add a quick splash of colour while perennial plantings mature. Some will self-seed in years to come.*

inherently less efficient herbaceous perennials, have to take second place, resulting in a carpet of grass with a sprinkling of wildflowers.

Gardeners have traditionally segregated 'grass' and 'flowers', whereas in the new perennial garden they are often mixed, hence the role that 'meadows' play in these gardens. However, we gardeners tend to want lots of wildflowers and only just

enough grass to create the sensation of an idealized country field where grass blades blow romantically in the breeze. On reasonably moist fertile soils, grasses tend to dominate, making the establishment of wildflowers difficult. On less fertile, drier soils — especially alkaline ones, on limestone and chalk — grasses do not grow so well, giving an opportunity for a very wide range of attractive and colourful wildflowers to

occupy a larger proportion of the ground. This is why wildflower gardeners prefer poor thin soils, and often try to reduce the fertility of richer soils.

Most gardeners who grow perennials know of several large or rather invasive plants that can become a nuisance in the border; *Macleaya cordata*, soapwort (*Saponaria officinalis*) and bistort (*Persicaria bistorta*, formerly *Polygonum bistortum*) are three. These can be put to good use in making meadows on fertile soils, as most of them are natives of moist fertile environments. A lawn can be converted to such a meadow by planting species such as these directly into grass. When large perennials dominate the result is often called a prairie garden. True prairie plants, though, are from central North America.

Even though there is no grass matrix in the open border, the inspiration here comes from the way that wildflowers in meadows grow together in loose groups. Such a planting is more like a conventional border than a meadow, and needs more maintenance — often to keep wild grasses out.

Meadows

MEADOWS – areas of grass allowed to grow long, liberally interspersed with wildflowers – are characteristic of the new perennial garden. Yet they are not a novel garden feature; gardeners started making them over a hundred years ago.

To some eyes a meadow is inherently untidy, too much an intrusion of the unordered world beyond the garden fence. And at certain times – autumn, perhaps, or after a summer storm which flattens the grass – they can indeed look dishevelled and scruffy. Yet various measures can be employed to make a meadow look 'intended' rather than just uncared for (see pages 18-19). Meadows are very often created away from the house and the main part of the garden, but this need not be the case. If surrounded by a border of mown grass and framed by other more conventional garden features, there is no reason why a meadow should not form a deliberate attraction right next to the house.

Quite apart from the wildflowers, there are a number of other aspects of meadows that make them a desirable garden feature. One is their soft haziness, the romanticism of grass that bends with every breeze, and the associations of pastoral landscapes that they conjure up. Unlike a border where we can see individual plants and the role they play in making the whole picture, in a meadow flowering plants lose their individuality, becoming more like threads in a Persian carpet. When one species stands out, however – a very tall plant, or a particularly architectural one – the contrast between this and the softness of the meadow background enhances the former's distinctive qualities.

An established meadow is undoubtedly low-maintenance, needing only a few cuts per year, perhaps only one. This in itself is reason enough to recommend it, especially on sites where access with mowers is difficult. Maintenance in the early stages is crucial, though, the routine in the first two years being far from labour-saving for the gardener (see pages 107-15).

One of the most attractive features of 'natural' meadows is the way that the

Simply allowing an area of grass to remain uncut for several months for a few years can result in wildflowers joining the grass. Here dandelions and ox-eye daisies make a bright late spring scene.

wildflowers (and the grasses, for that matter) are not scattered at random, but have concentrations of individuals that ebb and flow – here a cluster of buttercups, there a cluster of ragged robin – but always blending into each other. These higher concentrations of a particular species are often the result of subtle ecological factors; slightly more moisture in one place will enable the ragged robin, for example, to do somewhat better there. Otherwise they may be a reflection of the growth habit of a plant; *Monarda* species, for example, constantly expand outwards and die back in the centre, which leads to a pattern of individuals radiating out from a central point. A garden meadow will eventually show these sorts of patterns, as the plants jostle for position over the years, but you can also create these kinds of natural looking effects, to some extent, at the sowing or planting stages.

Just as different natural sites have different meadow plant communities, depending on factors such as the moisture and fertility of the soil and local climate, so the gardener needs to select an appropriate meadow plant community for the site to be developed. Fortunately the hard work of plant selection has been very largely done by the growers of meadow seed mixes, so it is possible to buy a grass/wildflower mix specifically composed for sandy soil, clay, poor drainage, thin chalk and so on. Some wildflowers are very adaptable: wild carrot (*Daucus carota*) and self-heal (*Prunella vulgaris*) are examples to be found in the majority of seed mixes. Others are more particular, and are included in fewer mixes. Meadowsweet (*Filipendula ulmaria*) survives grass competition only in damp soils in which it luxuriates, whereas its close relative dropwort (*F. vulgaris*) is the opposite, surviving the competition of other plants only on thin limestone soils.

The blue-violet Salvia pratensis *is one of the most prevalent and long-flowering wildflowers on limestone throughout Europe and is easy to establish in meadow gardens, as is the ox-eye daisy.*

Grasses and wildflowers for meadows

MEADOWS AND BORDERS ARE obviously very different, and to make a successful meadow it is vital to understand the nature of these differences. In a border, the gardener places plants where they are wanted and over the years they essentially stay where they are put. A meadow, on the other hand – whether sown from seed, planted or made from a converted lawn – affords the gardener nothing like as much control over the plants and their location. A meadow is a dynamic community. In this competitive, natural-type environment there is constant to-ing and fro-ing as some individuals seed themselves and then die out and other plants spread or creep to colonize new areas. One species may benefit from the weather one year, seed well and consequently spread. Another year may see conditions that do not favour its growth, so it gets partly displaced by the stronger performance of others. Although many perennials can be relied upon to stay in one place for many years, there are constant surprises as plants that thrived in the first few seasons become less common as the meadow matures, while others increase in number. Perhaps the ultimate pleasure is the arrival of unexpected new species altogether, brought in on the wind or by birds.

Good examples of this kind of change are provided by wild carrot (*Daucus carota*) and ox-eye daisy (*Leucanthemum vulgare*). Both of these tend to thrive in the first few years after a meadow is sown, often turning it white with their flowers in early summer. In later years they reduce considerably in numbers, sometimes vanishing altogether. The annual or biennial carrot dies after flowering, and so is dependent upon resowing itself; it competes best with grass on thin, dry soils. The perennial daisy is also short-lived and likewise does well on dry soils. If conditions provide reasonable moisture and fertility, the grasses win out. The only way to keep these two wildflowers on this kind of soil is to delay mowing until they have set seed, and then to disturb the soil in some way (such as by heavy raking), providing their seeds with a place to grow.

Grasses are the essential part of a meadow, the matrix in which everything else must grow. Meadow grasses are turf grasses, that is, they spread out sideways, rooting as they go, so forming the mat of interwoven stems that we know as turf. As you might imagine, this is an extremely effective means of covering the ground and makes it difficult for anything else to start to grow. It not only seals the surface against opportunist weeds (the disturbance tolerators of pages 10-11), but also makes the survival of less efficient perennials difficult. The better the conditions for grass

LEFT *An infertile sandy soil is a good basis for a wildflower-rich meadow, because grass growth will be weakened. Wild mignonette* (Reseda lutea), *poppies, ox-eye daisies and thrift* (Armeria maritima) *here flourish and seed amidst sparse grass.*

RIGHT *These two close-ups of a fifteen-year-old wildflower meadow on a dry limestone soil show a host of species springing up through the grass. Violet* Salvia pratensis *is surrounded by ox-eye daisies and bird's-foot trefoil* (left), *while magenta* Geranium sanguineum *and its paler relative* G. pyrenaicum *mingles with buttercups* (right).

growth, the harder it is for perennials to survive, unless they too are vigorous and competitive (like many marshland or prairie wild-flowers) or tall enough to soar above the grasses (as are the perennials from the American prairies). On poor, dry soils where grasses are unable to cover the ground so completely, there is more bare earth, which gives the major perennials a better chance of succeeding and also allows more opportunity for annuals and short-lived perennials (like the wild carrot and ox-eye daisy) to seed themselves in the plant community.

Although grasses may not be the part that especially attracts us, they are the element that really makes a meadow, and their selection is itself important. Grass species vary considerably in their competitiveness. Some are so strong-growing that they effectively stifle all but the most robust wildflowers and elbow out most other

grasses on fertile soils. The 'improved' varieties of agricultural rye grass (*Lolium* species) are the worst offenders from our point of view. Others are sufficiently competitive to make the survival of less vigorous wildflowers chancy, although it may be appropriate to use them on sites where there is a high risk of infestation of perennial weeds such as docks and nettles.

All good meadow mixes should be very roughly around three-quarters grass and one quarter wildflower seed, with the grasses consisting of relatively uncompetitive species which will co-exist happily with a wide variety of wildflower perennials even on moist, fertile soils. Read the list of ingredients before you buy. Suitable grasses include *Agrostis tenuis* (common bent or browntop), *Anthoxanthum odoratum* (sweet vernal grass), *Briza media* (quaking grass), *Cynosurus cristatus* (crested dog's-tail),

Festuca ovina (sheep's fescue), *F. rubra* (creeping fescue or red fescue), *Hordeum secalinum* (meadow barley), *Koeleria macrantha* (crested hair grass – suitable only for dry habitats), *Phleum pratense* (Timothy grass, cat's-tail), and *Trisetum flavescens* (yellow oat grass). For very rough sites where perennial weed competition is likely to be severe, or maintenance difficult, use *Alopecurus pratensis* (meadow foxtail, common foxtail – suitable for damp conditions), *Dactylis glomerata* (cocksfoot), *Deschampsia cespitosa* (tufted hair grass, tussock grass), *Festuca arundinacea* (tall fescue), *F. pratensis* (meadow fescue) and *Holcus lanatus* (Yorkshire fog).

It is feasible to increase the proportion of wildflowers to grasses and obtain more colourful results in the short term, but the reduced proportion of grasses may encourage greater weed penetration.

Wildflower lawns

WHILE MEADOWS LOOK BEST in a broad sweep, and so need medium or large-sized gardens, wildflower lawns are suitable for even postage-stamp sites. So long as the heaviest trampling is avoided they can be used as any other lawn – for sunbathing, games and entertaining.

The aim is to create a very short meadow, an area of grass that is kept at a slightly higher level than an average lawn, and mown less frequently. The majority of the wildflowers that will thrive in it are spring- and early-summer flowering. They will naturally have to be those species that are low-growing, of which there tend to be fewer as the year goes on. In addition they can include those species, including many bulbs, that are able to grow and flower earlier in the year than the grass and can be mown over later in their annual life-cycle when grass needs cutting more frequently.

You can start a wildflower lawn simply by reducing the cutting frequency on an existing lawn, raising the mower blades slightly, and seeing what comes up. (Remember to remove clippings to help reduce fertility.) Or you may start from scratch by sowing a seed mix of fine lawn grasses into which some of the appropriate wildflower seed has been mixed. Alternatively, turf can be used, and wildflower plants inserted in small holes. Over small areas lawns can be enriched by planting wildflowers directly into the ground. Seed may also be introduced into an existing lawn by scratching the surface with a rake and then sowing into the small bare patches that are exposed. This technique (known as scarification) is not so successful, as it is more difficult for seedlings to establish themselves.

It is important that any grass seed or turf used is made up from fine lawn grasses, with absolutely no ryegrass. More vigorous grasses will compete with the wildflowers too strongly. For the same reason no fertilizers should be used. Once it is established, a wildflower lawn needs cutting every few weeks, to a height of 8 cm/3 ½ in, leaving a pause of several weeks in early summer to allow seeding to take place. If spring bulbs and other flowers such as primroses and cowslips are a feature, then cutting will additionally have to be suspended from late winter to early summer.

The year in a wildflower lawn can start off with crocuses and snowdrops, moving on to chionodoxas and primroses, violets, anemones and the spring-flowering *Cyclamen repandum* in any shadier areas. The foliage of dwarf early-flowering bulbs dies down by late spring, which will not interfere too much with the cutting of grass. Primroses and violets can be cut once they have finished flowering, although it is better, in the interests of their spreading, to wait until they have seeded. A rotary cylinder mower should be used, set as high as possible. A colourful alternative to primroses are polyanthus hybrids, which can be used to create a most colourful effect in slightly shaded or moist spots. Cowslips are one of the most spectacular wildflower-lawn plants, with a long season, forming increasingly large colonies of yellow if allowed to seed.

Later on, in early summer, daisies (*Bellis perennis*) will be a major feature, reappearing occasionally throughout the

season. Germander speedwell (*Veronica chamaedrys*) will spread its tiny china-blue flowers through the grass, while cat's ear (*Hypochaeris radicata*), hawkbit (*Leontodon hispidus*) and bird's-foot trefoil (*Lotus corniculatus*) will all glow yellow. By mid-summer, the main show is over, although self-heal (*Prunella vulgaris*) can be relied on to show a strong violet through much of the later part of the summer. In the autumn, crocuses can be in flower again; be sure to choose true crocus species such as *Crocus nudicaule* and not colchicums, which are quite unsuitable for lawns.

On thin, somewhat alkaline and dry soils the variety of wildflowers can naturally become much wider, as seeds blow in on the wind and find a niche to colonize. Centaury (*Centaurium erythraea*) and restharrow (*Ononis repens*) are two that can take advantage of the weaker grass on such soils. On damp soils, where there is not too much foot traffic, bugle (*Ajuga reptans*) may be established; not only does it have attractive blue flowers in late spring, but also bronze-tinged evergreen foliage. In addition to these wildflowers, it is possible to experiment with a larger range of species such as dwarf thymes and low-growing rockery plants.

RIGHT *A damp area of lawn becomes a picture of complementary colours in spring when scattered with the mauve lady's smock* (Cardamine pratensis) *and the pale early daffodils* Narcissus 'Dove Wings'.

FAR LEFT *Spring bulbs such as these grape hyacinths are easy to naturalize in grass. They are growing alongside wild lesser celandine* (Ranunculus ficaria).

LEFT *Snake's head fritillary* (Fritillaria meleagris) *flourishes in either meadow grass or lawns, especially if the soil is damp.*

Perennials in rough grass

When creating a wildflower meadow we aim to establish a community of relatively uncompetitive grasses as an amenable home for perennials. But it may not always be possible to establish such grasses, or to give much time to maintenance once the initial planting is finished. Steep slopes and banks, areas full of tenacious, strong-growing grasses and weeds such as nettles and thistles may simply be too much work to clear to make way for a true meadow. In addition, if the soil is fertile and full of grass and weed seeds, there may be little hope for one. The best solution is to plant really tough, often large, perennials which will be able to compete with vigorous grasses and weeds on their own terms. A meadow of sorts will be the result – much coarser, perhaps, than the ideal but still potentially exuberantly colourful. This is the kind of planting that some garden designers call a prairie, although the plants may not all be true prairie species.

A rough grass planting can quickly develop into an unusual and colourful sight. The year in such a planting may start off with the more robust varieties of daffodils, which are strong enough to compete with grass early in the year and complete their growth before being overshadowed. In more conventional garden situations the dying foliage of bulbs is often an eyesore, with the additional disadvantage that it leaves an ugly yellow patch when the grass is eventually cut. With this kind of planting, however, the yellowing leaves will be hidden by early summer by the growth of surrounding perennials. Spring can also see comfrey (*Symphytum*) flowering enthusiastically in various shades of blue, pink and white, joined by red campion (*Silene dioica*) in any moist or partly shaded areas.

Later, in early summer, geraniums flower among the rising grass, in hummocks spangled with blue, pink, mauve or white flowers. Soapwort (*Saponaria officinalis*) with pink or white flowers forms extensive clumps after midsummer along with the robust stems and huge leaves of elecampane (*Inula*) high above the grass supporting clusters of finely petalled yellow daisies. The year ends spectacularly with yellow goldenrod and rudbeckia, mauve, lavender and white asters and the towering pink

This area of virtually unmanaged rough grass features sage and St John's Wort (Hypericum) *with a backing of* Phlomis russelliana, *all capable of competing with vigorous grasses. The phlomis leaves make an interesting visual contrast with the grass.*

heads of Joe Pye weed (*Eupatorium fistulosum* and related species).

The technique used to create such scenes is to plant in holes cut into the grass, and then to nurse the young plants through the first year or two. It is a technique that can also be used to create something closer to a true wildflower meadow, in areas of fine, less competitive grasses – established lawns, for instance. Alternatively, the perennials may be planted out and grass sown between them. The details of all these techniques are discussed on pages 112-3 and 118-9.

Vigorous grasses can take maximum advantage of the conditions that favour competitive plants – sun, fertile and moist soils – and climates where growth is possible during the winter. The only perennials that can compete successfully with them are those that are also able to take advantage of these favourable conditions. Some, such as yarrow (*Achillea millefolium*), field buttercup (*Ranunculus acris*) and many hardy geraniums, are evergreen and grow through the winter along with the grasses in regions where this is possible. Others, perhaps not evergreen, are able to compete because they grow taller than the grasses, over-shadowing them; these include species of *Inula* and *Solidago*.

The growth habit of many of these species often enables them to compete and displace

grasses and weaker plants. Some are clump-formers, steadily increasing in size; species of comfrey, for example, form extensive grass-excluding colonies. Others are able to swamp surrounding plants with their own growth, making them particularly effective as weed suppressants. One of the most effective plants at this is *Geranium × oxonianum* 'Claridge Druce'. It forms a dome-shaped hummock of foliage and flowers, which collapses soon after flowering time, taking surrounding grass and weeds down with it. From the centre then emerges

a new set of growth which will flower again in late summer. Yet other perennials are able to insinuate their way through tough surrounding vegetation with shoots that emerge some way from the parent plant – for example, soapwort.

Some of these strong-growing species self-seed easily, which may become a problem in the border or even in a wildflower meadow, but may be all too welcome in rough grass. *Aquilegia vulgaris* and *Alchemilla mollis* are two which can do this extensively.

Planted ten years ago, this area has not been touched since. Geranium 'Claridge Druce' *and hemerocallis varieties compete successfully with rough grasses at the outer perimeter of a garden, and leafy elecampane* (Inula racemosa) *prepares for a display of yellow daisy flowers later in the summer.*

Plantings in full sun

Day lilies (Hemerocallis) *are some of the most adaptable and deservedly popular of mid-summer flowering perennials. They are remarkably tolerant of a wide range of situations, sun or light shade and most soils, flourishing in both moist and 'average' moisture conditions. They grow well in rough grass and can naturalize. The larger flowered hybrids, such as these, are best kept in borders and relatively controlled plantings like this one; the smaller-flowered hybrids and species are more appropriate in wilder settings.*

The coreopsis in the foreground is one of another adaptable group of perennials. The lilac at the back is Campanula lactiflora, *a very large-growing species that looks equally good in both border and wild situations.*

Prairies

ALTHOUGH THE WORD PRAIRIE conjures up a vision of vast open spaces, prairie plantings are ideally suited to smaller gardens and more intimate landscapes. The tallest prairie plants are smaller than many of the oversized shrubs that dominate small gardens: many only reach a metre, or about three feet, at their maximum height. The height and bulk of prairie wildflowers can be used in a similar way to shrubs, but unlike shrubs, they will be at their maximum height only from midsummer to late autumn, or late winter if you cut them later in the year.

The great potential of prairie flowers lies in how easy they are to establish and the fact that they require little maintenance thereafter. The most attractive native European wildflowers grow on relatively infertile soils and are easily overrun by vigorous grasses and tenacious docks and thistles. In contrast, North American prairie plants are generally lusty growers that make the most of the nutrients available. Many grow at a rate which enables them to outpace even the fastest rye grass or dock.

The majority of prairie species flower in late summer to early autumn, which is an advantage since this is traditionally a dull season in gardens. Standing in a prairie garden in late summer, looking up at the tops of the Joe Pye weed (*Eupatorium*) and ironweeds (*Vernonia*) which were only just emerging from the ground four months before, brings home just what strong growers these plants are. Prairie plantings are therefore ideal for sites with a fertile soil, where the establishment and maintenance of less vigorous and sturdy wildflowers would be impractical.

Many different types of prairie can be created in the garden and there is an

enormous range of species to choose from. Just as an established meadow planting consists mainly of turf-forming grasses, which knit closely together to prevent invasion by weeds or dominance by one particular species, so a prairie planting must have a foundation of grasses, plants such as those of the pea family (*Lespedeza* and *Desmodium*), and daisy family like *Coreopsis*. Once this basic matrix has been established, invasive weeds are kept out, and it becomes possible to add smaller, less vigorous species such as spring-flowering *Dodecatheon meadia* and midsummer *Liatris pycnostachya*.

Inspired by the prairies, although much more conventional in its effect, is this magnificent herbaceous border. Grasses, including varieties of Miscanthus sinensis, *and the prairie wildflower* Eupatorium purpureum, *towering at the back of the border, form the permanent basis of the planting, while annual cosmos provides a splash of late summer colour. The perennials need only one winter cut-back, whereas the cosmos needs yearly resowing. This can be done straight into the ground in areas where late frost does not threaten.*

Prairie flowers in a suburban front garden are much more colourful than conventional lawns and ground cover in adjacent sites. Here, purple coneflower (Echinacea purpurea) *and yellow* Coreopsis *species in the foreground, and a pink bergamot* (Monarda fistulosa) *behind, create a bright splash of colour. Their strong hues do not clash, because they are seen as dots of colour on a neutral background of green grass. Although it would dilute the dramatic impact of the colours further, the addition of more grass species to the planting would make weed encroachment less likely.*

A small prairie area such as this will need only an annual cut-back; this is most easily performed with a strimmer. It can be done in the late autumn, if you like the garden to look tidy, or in late winter if you have species with attractive seedheads or wish to leave them for the birds. In areas with a cold winter climate, leave the trimmings covering the ground over winter.

A planting of ornamental grasses and perennials

F‌ROM MIDSUMMER UNTIL THE BEGINNING of the winter, grasses provide plenty of interest in this planting, situated on a bank between two grassy areas. It is very much an open border – a broad expanse of naturalistic planting that imitates the beauty of natural vegetation in the wild. The lower part of the planting has a reasonably moist, deep soil and is shaded late in the day by neighbouring trees. The upper part has a thin and stony soil that suffers the occasional summer drought and receives sun throughout the day.

The planting plan shows how the largest and most visually dominant plants, the grasses, are few in number and kept apart. The space between them in the upper, drier area is filled with perennials and wildflowers, which are of moderate competitiveness and whose colours are complementary.

The lower, damper area is planted with more strongly growing perennials, which form a continuous layer of foliage during the growing season, minimizing opportunities for weeds to encroach and to become established. Lower-growing or bushy perennials, such as the geranium and the astilbe, are planted along the verge to ensure a relatively tidy edge where the planting meets the grass. Leave the astilbe flowers, dried and brown, to continue interest through the autumn and into the winter months.

In addition to the plants shown on the planting plan, there are narcissi in the lower area and grape hyacinths (*Muscari armeniacum*) in the upper, both of which will flower in spring.

ABOVE Stipa gigantea, *with its dramatic fountain of flower stems, thrives on the drier, poorer soil in the upper part of the planting. It will create a major visual impact from midsummer through to autumn. The lower part, which has a deeper, moister soil, supports spectacular red astilbes and (on the right of the photograph) fluffy pink* Sanguisorba obtusa.

BELOW *In late summer, the grasses* Stipa gigantea *and* Deschampsia caespitosa *give a background of soft wildness to the striking mauve* Verbena hastata. *Both the verbena and the white* Verbascum chaixii *'Album' hybrid are sun-loving plants that will self-seed to some extent, scattering themselves around the garden without becoming a nuisance.*

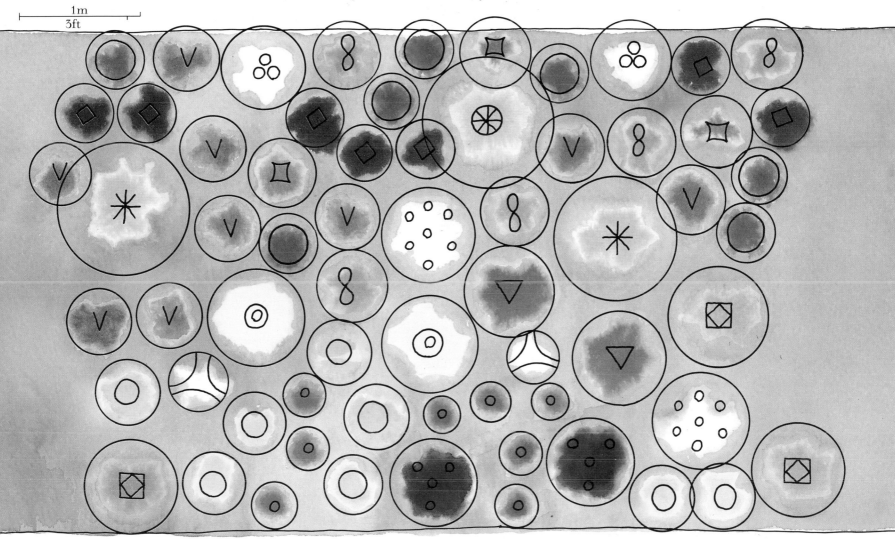

1m
3ft

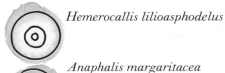 *Hemerocallis lilioasphodelus*

Anaphalis margaritacea

 Nepeta × racemosa 'Superba'

Verbascum chaixii 'Album'

Dianthus carthusianorum

 Astilbe chinensis var. *pumila*

 Deschampsia caespitosa

 Astilbe × arendsii 'Feuer'

 Iris unguicularis

 Verbena hastata

 Salvia pratensis

Stipa gigantea

 Astilbe × arendsii 'Irrlicht'

 Geranium 'Johnson's Blue'

 Sanguisorba obtusa

Solidago odora

73

Heathland

HEATH AND MOORLAND habitats are at once both bleak and colourful. Bleak because they are so often windswept and treeless; colourful because when seen from a distance the flowering heathers and russet grasses often form a mosaic of tones marking the different kinds of vegetation. Gardening in such an area can be problematic. The poor, acid soil is often accompanied by cold, windy conditions. Yet by concentrating on growing the natural flora of such an area, it is possible to create an attractive garden with much winter interest.

The characteristic vegetation of such areas consists of small, shrubby plants such as heathers (*Calluna vulgaris* and *Erica* species), dwarf rhododendrons and a host of plants that are related to them. Their leaves are nearly always evergreen and leathery and often very small, adaptations evolved to reduce water loss in the wind. The plants themselves have a tendency to grow together to form a solid mat of interwoven wiry stems. The advantage for the gardener is that this style of growth covers the ground with a permanent plant carpet of year-round interest. It is not surprising that these plants, heathers in particular, have become popular as a part of low-maintenance gardening in all areas. To thrive, though, they nearly all need to be grown on a soil which is acid or at least neutral (pH 6.5 to 7), although the winter-flowering heather *Erica carnea* is lime-tolerant.

Plants of this heather and rhododendron family (known botanically as the Ericaceae) have been joined in gardens by the New Zealand hebes, many of which grow in similar environments, although they are not so cold-tolerant. The hardiest species are those with leaves reduced to small scales, the colour of the foliage and the form of the plant being the main reason for growing them. Others, with more distinct leaves, have attractive flowers as well, generally white or mauve. The hebes are best suited to windy but mild climates, coastal and west-coast environments especially.

In the wild these low-growing shrubby plants tend to be interspersed with grasses, which may, indeed, form the dominant vegetation in some areas. Several are

Different heathland species find their ecological niche in the damp ground at the edge of a pond. Yellow bog asphodel (Narthecium ossifragum) *grows alongside the moisture-loving* Erica tetralix.

attractive enough to include in garden plantings, particularly forms of *Deschampsia flexuosa*, which has some of the most graceful and airy flower and seed-heads of any grass, and *Molinia caerulea*, a much more robust plant with bluish stems which turn red-brown in autumn. Many evergreen sedges also thrive in these habitats, the most attractive from the gardener's point of view being from New Zealand. The brown *Carex comans* and the highly distinctive yellow-brown tufts of *C. testacea* are among the best known of these.

The heathland year starts off with the various colour forms of *Erica carnea*, which can start flowering in midwinter. Spring tends to be dominated by low-growing rhododendrons, of which an enormous number of species and hybrids is available. Some of the hybrids may seem too exuberant for a natural-style garden, although some of the species are naturally showy, too. This time of year also sees the flowering of other related plants, most of which are a good deal more subtle, relying for their beauty on tiny bell-shaped flowers, which are usually white. The cassiopes are exquisite, with masses of flowers on stems set with scale-like leaves, but are suitable only for cool climates. There are many species of *Gaultheria*, *Arctostaphylos* and *Vaccinium* (all Ericaceae) which have attractive foliage, often a deep red in spring.

Summer is when the majority of heathers flower, with *Calluna vulgaris* pre-eminent. Their colour lasts until well into the autumn. This season is also enlivened by the berries of many of the dwarf shrubs just mentioned – vacciniums and various forms of

Flat expanses of heather (Calluna vulgaris) *have a perfect vertical counterpoint in junipers* (Juniperus communis). *This is the wild form of the heather; the planting could be varied by using other colour forms.*

gaultheria, including *Gaultheria mucronata* (formerly *Pernettya mucronata*), which has masses of berries in red, white or pink. The grasses are at their best now, too, crowned with attractive seed-heads.

Conventional plantings place these plants in blocks of a single variety. Our approach, however, is to group them loosely, flowing into one another as they would in nature. Most are of a similar height, so creating some vertical interest is important. Slow-growing dwarf conifers are often used in conventional gardens, but grasses are more appropriate for our purposes, looking less contrived as well as offering a welcome contrast of texture.

The open border

Traditionally, borders have a horizontal backdrop of some kind – a fence, wall or hedge – so they follow the boundaries of a garden, often surrounding a patch of grass in the middle. Such conventions have been overturned by the concept of the 'open border'. This is an expanse of naturalistic-style planting made up of undulating drifts of perennial flowers and grasses, either in the form of an island bed, or occupying the whole width of the garden with paths running through it. The overall effect of such a planting creates a far greater impact than the conventional lawn surrounded by narrow strips of planting.

Plants for the open border must be ecologically suited to the soil, light and other conditions of the garden. It is useful to make a shortlist of suitable plants and consider when they will flower and which of them can be used as structural and theme plants. Structural plants are chosen for their form and foliage rather than their flowers and colour. Theme plants lead the colour scheme for a month or so.

In conventional borders and island beds, the tallest plants are usually massed at the back of the border (or the centre of the island bed) with the shortest at the front (or the outside), resulting in a gradient of height. With massed plantings, a sensation of height is created by a number of carefully distributed taller structural plants, such as echinops and macleaya, scattered around the planting. Grasses are one of the most useful structural plants for this type of planting as they contribute height without occupying too much horizontal space. *Calamagrostis* × *acutiflora* 'Karl Foerster', with its bold upright stems, is an ideal structural plant, whose feathery heads provide winter interest. Bamboos are an evergreen alternative for moist soils, or use clipped box for a hint of formality.

When selecting lower-growing plants, you can create a strong effect by using theme plants to dominate the planting for a time. In the planting scheme on page 73, the striking *Verbena hastata* is the theme plant in the upper area from midsummer onwards, and the goldenrod (*Solidago*) is the theme plant in the lower part during the late summer months.

At first glance, such a dramatic sweep of planting looks as if it might involve more labour, but if the plants are carefully selected to suit the conditions of the site this should not be the case. The only essential maintenance job in an established planting of this kind is the annual cutting of dead stems from herbaceous plants, best carried out in late winter. If the soil is poor and dry, or if the garden suffers regular seasonal drought, choose stress-tolerant plants, such as lavender and thyme, which can endure harsh conditions. Such plants require minimal maintenance; they thrive without feeding or irrigation and there is no weed problem as the soil is too dry and infertile to encourage random growth.

Gardens with more assured moisture and fertility levels are likely to suffer from weed competition. For a truly low maintenance scheme, select plants which are competitive enough to hold their own against weeds and which mesh together to resist weed encroachment. Hardy geraniums are invaluable in this respect. The spread of weeds can also be limited by the use of mulches, to prevent their seedlings from germinating.

Exuberant pastel-hued lupins flourish in this informal 'open border'. They are intermingled with other strong-growing perennials, which overpower weeds and take care of themselves.

Rockery plantings

Holiday memories of alpines growing wild in the mountains may inspire the creation of a rockery at home. Frustratingly, though, this is the habitat that is most difficult to re-create, partly because the conditions in which alpines thrive are rarely found at lower altitudes, and partly because even the most skilled rockery builder can only ever construct a pale imitation of the real thing. In addition, rockery plantings often need a tremendous amount of maintenance. Alpines are small and particularly vulnerable to being overrun by weeds and larger garden perennials, and removing weeds that have rooted around stones is one of the most difficult garden jobs.

Perhaps the best way to grow the smaller alpines is in raised beds, where a reasonably satisfying kind of miniature landscape may be created. Larger ones can be planted in a 'steppe' habitat (see pages 100-01), perhaps around a few rocks positioned to vary the immediate landscape rather than to imitate nature. Often, however, you find yourself dealing with an existing rockery that is already an established feature in a garden. If the removal of even the most dreadful pile of stones and rubble (which many of them are) is too daunting, it is best to concentrate on hiding the unsightly feature. Choose the more robust and vigorous alpines and other low-growing plants that can stand up to weed seedlings and are able to compete effectively with each other. In the end the use of such plants, which will rapidly overrun bare soil and start to mingle with each other, will probably do more to create a natural-looking garden feature than any amount of stonework.

The key to rockery planting is to understand and exploit all the micro-habitats that even the smallest one offers. A side that faces the sun offers a very different environment from a side that is in constant shadow, even though it may be less than a metre away around a corner. A slope facing the sun — especially if surrounded by rocks — will become considerably hotter than an adjacent piece of level ground. Such spots are ideal for succulents such as species of *Sedum* and houseleeks (*Sempervivum*), for Mediterranean-climate plants like the yellow *Hypericum olympicum*, late flowering origanums and wild thymes (*Thymus*), and for bulbs like tulips that need a good summer baking to make them flower again next season.

The shady side can support plants that could quite likely be killed by a few days on the sunny side. There is a considerable variety of miniature ferns, many of which flourish in the cracks in old walls. Two examples are *Asplenium trichomanes* with delicate fronds and the rusty-back fern *Asplenium ceterach*. Among flowering plants the finest must be the ramondas, which are related to the African violets we grow as houseplants; although regarded as choice alpines, they are in fact extremely long-lived and durable.

The richest natural flora is to be found on limestone, and yet alkaline rock is not essential for the successful cultivation of lime-loving plants. However, a high pH is anathema to those alpines that thrive in

Sedums such as Sedum rupestre *are among the most adaptable rockery plants, useful for their ability to tolerate drought and to grow in situations where soil is practically non-existent.*

nature on acidic rock such as granite or some sandstones — most dwarf rhododendrons and related plants, for example.

Much can be told about whether a plant is suitable for a low-maintenance naturalistic rockery from its habit of growth. The classic alpine cushion plant is usually too slow-growing, or too exacting in its requirements, to flourish with little care, rapidly falling victim to weed infestation. Those forming distinct rosettes with plenty of evidence of young ones sprouting around the side are usually more vigorous — sempervivums and the shade-loving London pride (*Saxifraga × urbium*) are two examples. Those with a sprawling habit, forming a tight mat of growth, are usually a safe bet although the odd one is terribly invasive, such as the common *Cerastium tomentosum*. A ground-hugging shrubby habit is quite frequent among mountain plants, and since the vast majority are evergreen, this makes them useful. Another growth habit that indicates that a plant is probably well able to look after itself is a tendency to sucker, where new growth is produced from underground shoots some distance from the parent plant, such as with *Campanula rotundifolia*.

Rockeries are undeniably at their best in the earlier part of the year, with small bulbs such as various dwarf narcissi and tulips, herbaceous perennials like pasque flowers (*Pulsatilla*), gentians and miniature shrubs, of which the heavily fragrant and lime-loving daphnes are the finest. Summer sees rock roses (*Helianthemum*), dianthus and phlox providing plenty of colour in the earlier months, but after midsummer it is increasingly difficult to find good plants.

The white form of valerian (Centranthus ruber *var.* albus) *thrives among bearded irises and rockery plants on a soil that consists of little more than gravel. It will also grow out of walls.*

Short-lived perennials, biennials and annuals

THE ADVANTAGE OF ANNUALS is both that they are very colourful and that they mature quickly, the nearest thing to instant gardening. They may not be perennials, but they do have a place in a natural-style garden. After all, many natural habitats have a permanent contingent of annuals as well as perennial species. Dry areas with thin soils have particularly rich annual floras. While the bedding plants that are very much a feature of the traditional summer garden involve a lot of labour in raising and planting out, the annuals for our kind of gardening can be sown directly into the ground where they are to flower, and in some cases will seed themselves to reappear next year.

In addition to annuals, this category includes a number of short-lived perennials that usually survive for only a few years at most, for example the bright cerise *Lychnis coronaria* and the scented sweet rocket or dame's violet (*Hesperis matronalis*). Others, such as the silvery thistle-like *Eryngium giganteum*, live for two or more years, flower once and then die. Such plants invariably set large quantities of seed which germinates easily, often enabling them to survive for many generations in the garden.

The annuals appropriate to the new perennial garden are mostly colourful yet subtle. Many of them, like love-in-the-mist (*Nigella damascena*) and 'poached eggs' (*Limnanthes douglasii*), were popular in traditional cottage gardens. Others are newer to cultivation, but have been selected by seed merchants as an alternative to the brash colours of conventional bedding annuals. A much-loved group consists of the 'weeds' of old-fashioned cornfields, now all but eliminated by modern herbicides and seed-cleaning methods, and includes field poppies (*Papaver rhoeas*) and corncockle (*Agrostemma githago*).

Annuals add an undeniable splash of colour to a planting, which is especially useful when the garden is newly planted out and there are gaps that need to be filled temporarily. Since they have to reproduce themselves before the year is out in order to keep the species going, annuals produce proportionately more flowers than do perennials, which can always live to seed again another year. They are consequently often extremely floriferous and intensely colourful, which is why they have always been popular with gardeners.

As well as growing annuals in gaps between perennials, it is possible to create dramatically colourful beds planted with nothing but annuals. So long as the soil is reasonably free of weeds, little work is needed between sowing the seed and clearing away the dead plants in autumn. There will, however, be little to look at through the winter months. The cornfield wildflower planting is a particular form of this kind of bed and is perhaps the most colourful of all, although field poppies do not stay in flower for more than a few weeks. For a longer-lasting display sow the seeds in succession – a new area every few weeks in the spring – much as vegetable growers sow lettuce to ensure successive crops through the season.

Cornfield and other annual plantings are rarely permanent. As disturbance tolerators they need bare soil in which to grow, and are rapidly displaced by grass and other perennial plants. Only on very dry soils, where there is incomplete vegetation cover, can you expect to have some coming up every year. They are thus dependent on some cultivation, with an annual tilling of the soil to ensure that the autumn's scattered seeds are given a place to grow.

Short-lived perennials are often intensely coloured like the annuals, or they may have other, more sculptural qualities, as does *Eryngium giganteum*, for example. Its name, 'Miss Willmott's ghost' comes from the renowned English gardener's habit of surreptitiously scattering seed in the gardens she visited. Another is the caper spurge (*Euphorbia lathyrus*), which often appears in gardens where it has never been planted, and supposedly deters moles. These plants readily self-seed on bare soil.

Part of the charm of these perennials is this habit of self-sowing where they please. By deciding themselves where they are going to grow they add that important element of insouciance and naturalness that can be difficult to achieve by design alone. In conventionally planted borders, or open borders, where there is usually some annual cultivation of the soil to remove weeds they are often able to self-sow sufficiently every year to keep going. You need to make sure that your weed control tactics, either by hoeing or by using mulches, are not so effective that these self-seeders cannot be given a chance to grow. Just occasionally seedlings might come up in an inconvenient spot such as the middle of a path, but then you can pull them out.

In meadows and other wild-garden habitats it is more difficult, but not impossible, for these plants to keep on sowing themselves in what are almost closed plant communities. If you want large drifts, they will have to be given some help, perhaps by annual sowing in small gaps created especially for them.

Yellow corn marigold, blue cornflower, mauve corncockle, poppies and chamomile are colourful old-fashioned cornfield annuals. They are short-lived, but make a spectacular start to a wildflower garden.

Plantings for waterside and damp ground

D AMP GROUND SHOULD BE SEEN as a marvellous opportunity for gardeners to grow the vigorous, exuberant and colourful plants typical of natural wetlands rather than as a problem site calling for the effort and expense of drainage. People lucky enough to have a lakeside or streamside garden can take advantage of the damp conditions in its vicinity to enhance the romantic qualities of such a situation. Those without can draw on a wide range of materials and equipment – from the simple to the technologically advanced – to create a pond or bog garden. With appropriate planting, even artificial water features can very quickly be made to seem natural and will begin to play an important part in local ecology.

Damp ground and a tolerably fertile soil provide ideal conditions for the most lush – even exotic – plantings, where strong contrasts of leaf shape and flower form can be developed. The large rounded leaves of Ligularia veitchiana *are a foil for its yellow flower spikes, and both contrast with the mauve feathery heads of* Sanguisorba obtusa. *The tall deep purple plant is* Angelica gigas, *a biennial that readily self-sows.*

Plantings for waterside and damp ground

Wetlands are obviously lush environments. Constant moisture allows plants to grow without interruption through the growing season, and to some extent can make up for lack of soil fertility. Not only does vegetation flourish luxuriantly, often graced with much larger leaves than that of drier places, but such a productive environment attracts a wide range of animal life. In summer the air near water is usually humming with insects, which in turn attract birds, amphibians and reptiles. Wetlands are vital wildlife habitats, and their destruction by drainage has depleted the numbers of many species. Thus creating a garden wetland — even just a small pond or boggy area, contained in a butyl rubber pond liner and artificially kept moist — has real value to local ecology. And surrounding a pool with marshland plants not only creates a multitude of habitats, but also provides a visual context for the water. It helps the feature look natural, as opposed to the obviously artificial garden pond with no transition zone to surrounding dry land. If you are considering installing any kind of water feature it is worth thoroughly researching the subject. Consulting experts and specialized books will not only give you ideas on design, construction and planting, but will help you deal with water supply and drainage.

A walk through a natural wetland reveals a fascinating and highly visible mosaic of different plant communities — here a foaming mass of meadowsweet (*Filipendula ulmaria*), there a cluster of the yellow flowers of greater spearwort (*Ranunculus lingua*), often with quite clear lines of demarcation where one dominant or eye-catching species ends and another takes over. These patterns result from the tendency of certain plant species to dominate over others in areas of different soil moisture content. When planning your garden wetland, it is thus important to match plants to the soil moisture levels.

Most plants will grow better if given constant rather than intermittent moisture, so long as the soil is not waterlogged (and

The giant rhubarb, Gunnera manicata, *is the most tropical-looking plant that can be grown in a cool climate. Grown in moist soil alongside ferns, hostas and* Ligularia stenocephala, *it conjures up a jungle atmosphere.*

thus lacking in oxygen). Vigorous species are best able to take advantage of such conditions, soon elbowing aside any slower-growing neighbours. Wetter ground closer to the water table – where air is excluded from the soil – is unfavourable to the growth of many plants, and only species particularly adapted to these waterlogged conditions will thrive. In some cases these are plants that will not grow well in drier environments – the flowering rush (*Butomus umbellatus*) for instance; other examples such as many bog irises (the yellow *Iris pseudacorus* and the blue-violet *I. sibirica* and *I. versicolor* among them), are happy in either, but in nature are found only in wet habitats. Other more specialized water plants – marginals or aquatics – grow or float in the water itself, and some will have preferences for different depths of water.

The key to getting the most out of a garden wetland, both visually and ecologically, is to provide gradients of wetness rather than sudden changes. Where the whole spectrum of soil moisture – everything between open water and dry land – is available for colonization by as wide a range of plants and animals as possible, each one is able to find its ecological niche. A damp meadow area will support a mixture of meadow perennials and plants that grow particularly well with abundant moisture. As the moisture level rises, the marshland plants take over. With waterlogging, the variety of species will change again until the water's edge is reached, where marginal plants able to grow in the soil under the

water will thrive. In open water there are free-floating plants like duckweeds (*Lemna* species), those that are rooted in the bottom with floating leaves and flowers, such as waterlilies (*Nymphaea* and *Nuphar*), and those which are almost entirely submerged, such as water violet (*Hottonia palustris*), which shows only its flowers above water. In the garden only a few metres or yards are necessary to develop a gradient like this.

Because damp ground favours vigorous, rapidly spreading plants, there is the potential danger of introducing into the wild extremely invasive plants which can displace native species or even clog waterways. An example is purple loosestrife (*Lythrum salicaria*), a spectacularly colourful and perfectly well-behaved denizen of European

marshland. In the USA and Canada it has become rampant, possibly because of a lack of local predators, to the extent that its cultivation has been banned in some states.

While most wetlands are fertile, those on poor acid soils are not. The resulting habitat, known as bog, can be hostile to plant life. The specialized plants that flourish there are nevertheless often as attractive – if not as luxuriant – as those of more fertile wetlands. They include several insectivorous genera such as sundews (*Drosera*), pitcher plants (*Sarracenia*) and butterworts (*Pinguicula*). Even a tiny area of bog in a heathland garden can support a rich variety of these interesting plants and provide a striking contrast with surrounding heathers and other dwarf shrubs.

Ferns, generally thought of as shade-lovers, tolerate more open conditions if the soil is moist enough. Here the royal fern, Osmunda regalis, *is growing in a damp ditch alongside a rodgersia.*

Damp ground plantings

Damp ground can be defined as ground where water does not drain away during periods of continuous rain, or which remains moist through periods when other parts of the garden become dry in summer. It may be only seasonally wet, usually during the winter, which may restrict the choice of plants to those that are able to tolerate waterlogging when they are dormant. Ground that is damp through most of the summer as well, though, provides the best conditions for a wide variety of wetland plants.

The whole of your garden may be damp, or only certain patches. In the case of the latter, a marshland planting may be incorporated into a feature such as a meadow, with a subtle change in the flora as the ground becomes wetter. However you arrange the young plants or sow the seed when you make the garden, the plants themselves will eventually decide their own growing places, the moisture-loving species working out their own boundaries as against those plants that need drier soils.

The year in a damp meadow starts slowly. Given that they can grow continuously through the growing season, most moisture-lovers leave it until late before flowering. Lady's smock (*Cardamine pratensis*) is an early exception, its flowers of subtlest lavender appearing from otherwise invisible little plants to carpet the ground in spring. Soon after, red campion (*Silene dioica*) can make a colourful spectacle. This plant illustrates well how readily available soil moisture may compensate for stronger light conditions than are usually tolerated. Normally a dweller in partial shade, red campion is happy enough in full sunlight

provided the soil never dries out.

Later, in early summer, the globe flowers appear; *Trollius* species and varieties in orange, yellow and cream are plants characteristic of damp, open meadows and very amenable to garden cultivation. Also at this time meadow rues (*Thalictrum* species) come into their own, their tall shoots making remarkably fast progress before bursting into fluffy panicles of pink or cream flowers. The larger Asiatic primula species are a possibility, too, for this season. They are among the most colourful candidates for moist shade, but given a reliably damp soil they will flourish equally in sun. The longest-lived and most reliable is the sturdy Himalayan cowslip (*Primula florindae*), whose yellow flowers give off a delicious spicy scent.

All the plants mentioned so far are happiest on reasonably fertile, slightly acid to alkaline soils. On less fertile, acid soils the selection of species may be poorer, but is still potentially colourful. Among the best combinations for such places are the pink-flowered marsh orchids *Dactylorhiza incarnata* and *D. majalis*, with pale yellow *Rhinanthus serotinus*, an annual semi-parasite on grasses. The orchids will often arrive of their own accord in areas where they grow wild, as their almost microscopic seed travels long distances. The rhinanthus will have to be sown initially, but usually self-sows subsequently and, being an annual, will constantly change its position with each year. Incidentally, the smaller yellow rattle (*Rhinanthus minor*) is a useful plant for dry meadows, and both sap the strength of vigorous grasses, thus encouraging other wildflowers.

By mid- to late summer the number of plants in flower will increase. Many are very colourful, such as magenta-toned purple loosestrife (*Lythrum salicaria*), yellow loosestrife (*Lysimachia vulgaris*) or scarlet

cardinal flower (*Lobelia cardinalis*). Among such bright colours a visual buffer is useful, and what better plant for this purpose than meadowsweet (*Filipendula ulmaria*), whose creamy, fluffy flowers are such a feature of summer on damp ground all over Europe? Despite its vigorous nature and tendency to seed itself around, it never becomes a nuisance; its slender, non-spreading habit means that it never threatens to overwhelm more delicate neighbours. Similar in effect is valerian (*Valeriana officinalis*), which is also tall and slender with white or pink flowers.

The finest late-summer and autumn plants for damp places tend to be from North America – the lobelia species already mentioned, the Joe Pye weeds (*Eupatorium purpureum* and related species) and the ironweeds (*Vernonia* species). The Joe Pyes are vast, magnificent specimen plants, shrub-like in their height and bulk and attracting prodigious numbers of butterflies. The ironweeds are tall and potentially somewhat leggy plants, but all with most attractive rich violet flowers.

Most ferns are best in moist shade, but some will flourish in more open conditions where the soil is wet enough. The royal fern (*Osmunda regalis*) is one of most outstanding herbaceous foliage plants, its lobed fronds building up into a sizable clump, best appreciated when surrounded by lower-growing plants.

Since they can grow all summer, with no fear of drying out, most moisture-loving plants tend to leave flowering until late. This waterlily-packed ornamental canal is surrounded by a thick growth of queen of the prairie (Filipendula rubra 'Venusta'), Sanguisorba hakusanensis *and pink and white* S. tenuifolia 'Alba'.

Waterside and aquatic plantings

T HE WATERSIDE ITSELF — the edge of a pond, lake or stream — provides a home for those plants that need or do well with water permanently at their roots. We can combine consideration of very marshy habitats with the waterside, as both have year-round water at or not far below the surface of the soil. Many of the plants in the table on pages 148-9 flourish in these very wet conditions, but do check that they are suitable for your climate. Some damp-lovers are intolerant

of waterlogging throughout the winter: bulbous plants like lilies and camassias are especially susceptible. Other marshland plants are frozen solid throughout winter in their homeland and may not flourish in milder wet winters. The spectacular scarlet *Lobelia cardinalis* is the best example of this, rotting off when grown in wet places where winters are mild.

Pond surroundings

Still water often has a fringe of growth that blurs the distinction between land and water. Often this consists of grassy plants like reeds (*Phragmites australis*), sweetgrass (*Glyceria maxima*), bur-reeds (*Sparganium*

Deliciously scented yellow Primula florindae *and yellow and red mimulus are amongst the easiest plants to establish for early and midsummer waterside colour, often self-seeding when happy.*

species) and reedmaces or cat's-tails (*Typha* species). Most of these tend to be large and vigorous, although smaller ones are available (such as *Typha minima*). More than anything else they add romance and a feeling of naturalness to a water planting. There is nothing like the sight and sound of a breeze rustling its way through a bed of reeds, all the flower heads bending and bowing simultaneously.

With or without grassy-leaved companions, plenty of attractive flowering plants suit waterside situations. Kingcups (*Caltha palustris* and related species) are invaluable for early spring, flowering exceptionally early for a waterside plant. Skunk cabbages (*Lysichiton* species) follow on a little later, large arum-lily-shaped flowers emerging from the mud before their vast leaves. Although they might be considered too large and rampant (and skunk-smelling) for some gardens, they are useful in situations where something is needed to hold muddy banks together. Even better for this kind of erosion control is *Darmera peltata*, a plant that sends up pale pink flower heads on tall stems in spring, followed by exotic-looking circular leaves. Its thick rhizomes are extremely effective at binding together unstable banks.

Later in the year there are moisture-loving irises, such as yellow flag (*Iris pseudacorus*) and a number of species in blue-violet shades such as *I. versicolor* and *I. ensata*. Several vigorous buttercup relatives thrive in waterside environments, such as *Ranunculus lingua* and *R. septentrionalis*. Most of these waterside plants tend to be bold rather than subtle, yet for smaller ponds there are plants that benefit from closer examination. There is the delicate pink of flowering rush (*Butomus umbellatus*), for example, which thrives in acid water, or the beautifully fringed white flowers of bogbean (*Menyanthes trifoliata*), which benefits from being able to grow without the competition of larger plants.

Waterlilies and other truly aquatic plants add an extra dimension to bodies of water, and perform a useful function in pond ecology by creating shade from the sun for fish and other water creatures. Wild waterlilies (*Nymphaea* and *Nuphar* species) tend to be very vigorous and widely spreading, too large for many ponds. Fortunately there are plenty of smaller cultivars and hybrids to choose from, some even small enough for a mini-pond in a half barrel on the patio. Selecting a variety should be done carefully, though, as many have an undeniably exotic quality and will look inappropriate in a naturalistic environment. Along with waterlilies there are other much smaller aquatics such as species of *Persicaria* and *Potamogeton*. Although less spectacular, these help to give a pond that natural look and are often valuable as food sources for birds and invertebrates.

Drifting plants
Free-floating aquatic plants root straight into the water and consequently drift about with changes in wind direction. Some are attractive in their own right, as well as being something of a curiosity. The fern *Azolla caroliniana* is one of the best, turning pinky red in the autumn. Such plants often appear spontaneously, being introduced unintentionally with other aquatic plants or even on waterbirds' feet, and can be invasive.

Submerged, and therefore largely invisible, aquatics may not seem an important part of designing a pond, but they too have a role to play as oxygenators, part of the food web and as hiding places for innumerable insects and invertebrates. Even if we never see them – and mostly we will not – these creatures provide food for larger animals like amphibians and birds. Some submerged plants such as the graceful water violet or the water crowfoots (*Ranunculus* species) produce flowers above water. Submerged aquatics can reproduce themselves rapidly, sometimes too rapidly, often growing new plants from bits of broken-off stem. The Canadian pondweed (*Elodea canadensis*), for

Flag irises grow in practically any wet ground, the purple orchids (Dactylorhiza majalis) *only on acid soils.*

example, has made itself singularly unwelcome in many a smaller pool.

Vigorous species
Caution needs to be exercised when choosing plants for aquatic environments, since conditions favour the unrestricted growth of vigorous plants, which can lead to small ponds becoming choked with one particular species in a short time. If you are planting a body of water that is part of a waterways system, rather than an isolated pool, then you have a responsibility to those downstream, and vigorous non-native plants should be avoided. Even if you have only a small body of water, you will not want to be constantly curbing the excesses of rampageous species. It is wisest to consult specialist books or nurseries dealing with aquatic plants and to talk to someone familiar with local conditions for advice on plants to choose and to avoid.

89

Waterside and damp ground planting should celebrate the fertility of the habitat. The sanguisorbas, filipendulas and astilbes here need plenty of water to do well. The hemerocallis and astrantias are not so dependent on a damp site, but do grow that much better when they find abundant moisture. The inclusion of moisture-loving grasses helps to create the atmosphere of reedy lushness that always characterizes natural marshland.

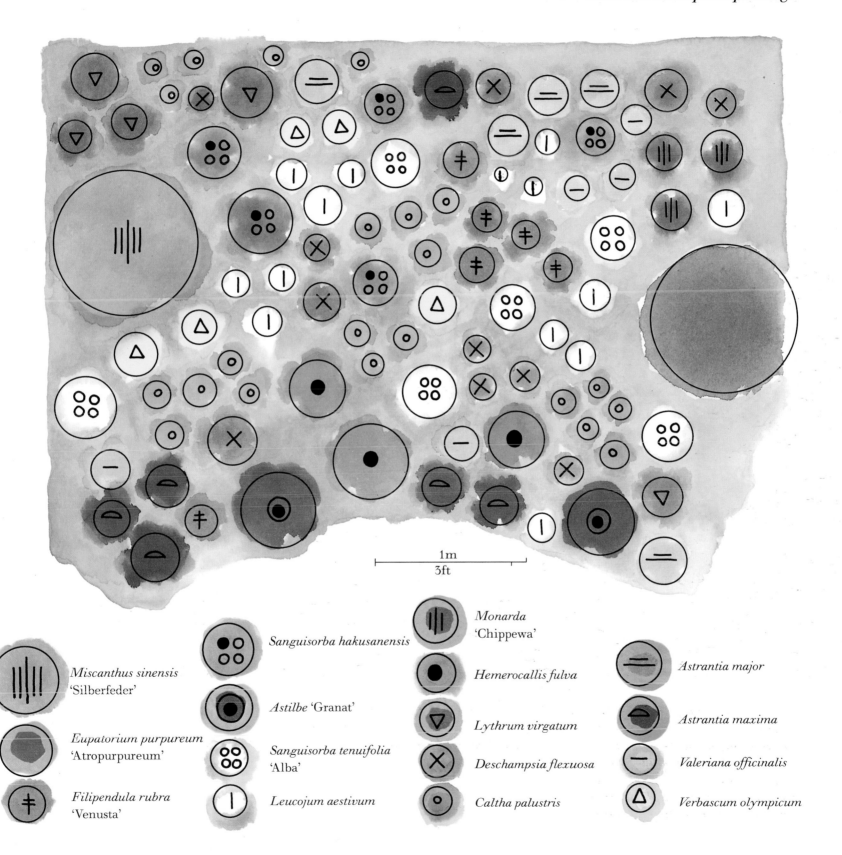

1m
3ft

		Monarda 'Chippewa'
Miscanthus sinensis 'Silberfeder'	Sanguisorba hakusanensis	Hemerocallis fulva
Eupatorium purpureum 'Atropurpureum'	Astilbe 'Granat'	Lythrum virgatum
Filipendula rubra 'Venusta'	Sanguisorba tenuifolia 'Alba'	Deschampsia flexuosa
	Leucojum aestivum	Caltha palustris

Monarda 'Chippewa'

Hemerocallis fulva

Lythrum virgatum

Deschampsia flexuosa

Caltha palustris

Astrantia major

Astrantia maxima

Valeriana officinalis

Verbascum olympicum

Plantings for dry areas

WE THINK OF WATER AS ESSENTIAL FOR PLANTS, and of its absence as inimical to their growth. Great efforts have been made throughout history to bring water to the desert and to create gardens that are fresh green oases in dry landscapes. Yet the irony is that gardens in dry areas can be extraordinarily colourful and rich in species without going to these lengths. In fact, it could be argued that a garden in a dry region can have more variety and colour in it than a garden in an area more favoured by the rains. First we need to explore the reasons for this paradox and then to consider how we can make the most of the great variety of plant life that thrives without irrigation.

Dry need not mean colourless, as is shown by the glowing profusion of bearded iris and valerian (Centranthus ruber) *in this Mediterranean garden. Irises come in a wide colour range, but their spectacular flowers are, unfortunately, short-lived. Valerian, however, has one of the longest flowering times of any dry-habitat plant.*

Plantings for dry areas

Until recently the emphasis when planting dry areas has been to irrigate the ground sufficiently to be able to grow what might be called 'the standard range of garden plants', nearly all of which require more water to flourish than is available locally. This desire for verdant green lawns, rose beds and rhododendron borders has placed huge demands on water resources that are becoming increasingly difficult to meet. It is not surprising that gardeners in areas of regular seasonal drought are turning more and more to look at plants that grow naturally in such conditions rather than those requiring constant irrigation. Recent decades have seen a burgeoning interest in growing native plants in both Australia and California – areas in which traditionally the beautiful local flora was scorned and only European imports grown in gardens.

Even in regions which have not been considered drought-prone, gardeners are having to rethink their planting practices. Pressure on water resources, worries about changing climate and successions of hot summers leading to hosepipe bans, are all forcing people to wonder about using water-hungry plants. Above all else the lawn – that hallmark of suburban civilization – is no longer being taken for granted. US plant breeders may work overtime on producing drought-resistant lawn grasses, but many gardeners now question the central importance of a lawn in the garden in the first place.

Dealing with drought

The key to gardening in drought-prone areas is to select plants that grow naturally in such environments. The vigorous competitive species of constantly moist soils will not thrive, whereas more slowly growing stress-tolerant plants will flourish. This reduced competition effectively means that a wider range of plants can be grown in a low-maintenance regime – a definite plus for the dry-land gardener.

In areas which have serious and regular droughts – those with a Mediterranean climate (hot, dry summers and cool, moist winters), for example – the emphasis should be on planting the best of locally native plants. These will have been 'tried and tested' by nature itself. They can be augmented by suitable introduced varieties for extra colour and interest. People who garden in dry pockets in moister regions –

In dry areas where irrigation needs to be minimized, drought-tolerant shrubs furnish colour and interest. Aromatic Lavandula stoechas *with purple flower spikes makes a pleasing contrast with yellow* Dendromecon rigida, *a poppy relative.*

those on very sandy soils or hot dry banks – need to base their plant selection on dry environments that are comparable in terms of temperature, avoiding the temptation to get carried away with tender exotics.

Plant habit varies a great deal with climate. Very dry, desert environments tend to have very specialized plant forms, often succulents, whose intriguing plastic shapes lend themselves to dramatic planting schemes. Regions with a Mediterranean climate have a preponderance of low, shrubby evergreen plants, with occasional taller trees. Many of our best-known garden plants are of this type; lavender (*Lavandula* species), myrtle (*Myrtus communis*), sage (*Salvia officinalis*) and ceanothus are good examples. Herbaceous perennials are relatively infrequent – it takes too much water to produce all that lush foliage every year; plants find it better to grow slowly and to shed as little as possible. Bulbs, though, can be a major feature; the richest bulb floras in the world come from dry climates – South Africa, the Mediterranean basin and Central Asia. These bulbs can grow, flower and seed during the cool moist season and then disappear into the comparative cool of the earth when the sun bakes the land in summer.

The other plant form that is very charac-teristic of both desert and Mediterranean climates is the annual. The ability to concertina a life-cycle – to respond to rain, germinate, flower and seed in a short period of time – is one way to survive in hot, dry areas. Masses of annual flowers (although very popular with many gardeners) can look out of place in temperate climates, their strong colours appearing garish in the softer light of higher latitudes. Yet such brilliant displays are completely natural in many desert regions. Indeed, the world's brightest floral spectacles are certain desert areas shortly after rain.

*Strong colours seem to be a definite feature
of dry-habitat plants. Here pink* Dianthus
carthusianorum *is complemented by a haze
of mauve nepeta (left) and silvery eryngium
(rear, centre) during midsummer. The grass,*
Pennisetum orientale, *will keep its feathery
heads until autumn.*

Dry-land plantings

Regions with Mediterranean-type climates have a kind of vegetation which is characteristically composed of low evergreen shrubs, with grasses, herbaceous plants and bulbs playing subsidiary roles. The shrubs often have distinctly greyish leaves, a function of the outer layer of fine hairs or wax coating that helps to prevent water loss. This, incidentally, is an attractive feature in itself, making them desirable as garden foliage plants even before flowers are considered. The very fact that they are evergreen is an additional bonus. The majority of these shrubs flower in early summer, before the sun is at its height. As garden plants they are useful in that they tend to have compact shapes, many being definitely ground-hugging. Gardeners can use them for covering large areas of soil with a blanket of attractive foliage.

While their origin may be in relatively warm climates, many of these shrubs are reasonably hardy and can be grown anywhere where the winter temperature does not fall below −10°C/14°F. This makes them useful plants for dry gardens in cooler climates, especially on steeply sloping sites that face the sun, which are often inhospitable to the normal run of garden plants and difficult to maintain.

The lavenders are among the best known of these low shrubs, their scent and grey foliage being as valued as their violet flowers. Similar to them in terms of the effect created by masses of tiny leaves are artemisias and santolina. The cistuses are another highly rated group, with open, thin-petalled flowers with a texture rather like crepe paper. Some, such as *C. × cyprius*, grow into quite large and open shrubs of 1.5 m/5 ft across, while others, like *C. salviifolius*, are lower and more compact.

The larger-flowered species and varieties are among the most spectacular flowers of the Mediterranean flora. A different kind of flower impact is created by varieties of ceanothus, mostly from western North America. Instead of a display of individual flowers, the tiny florets are packed into dense heads that smother the bushes at flowering time. Most are blue, and they can be overwhelmingly beautiful. The glossy foliage of many varieties is attractive, too.

Foliage is an important element to consider when selecting and combining these shrubs. Many subtle contrasts can be made using foliage alone. As well as the tendency to grey and silver colouring already mentioned, the need to conserve water led many plants to develop leaves that are very small and fine, or narrow and needle-like. The impact of a mass of such leaves from a distance is often of a hazy, matt-textured blur of subtle colour.

A disadvantage with many of these shrubs is that they appear to be quite short-lived. They also seem to become rather gangly with age. It may be that their short-lived nature is a problem of cultivation rather than inherent in the plant, as in gardens they are usually grown in higher nutrient conditions than they would find in the wild, growing unnaturally fast and possibly 'burning themselves out'. The poor shape of older plants can often be improved by hard pruning, and regular annual pruning after flowering can also help keep plants compact. Fortunately, nearly all are easily propagated by cuttings, so that plantings are easily renewed when necessary.

Bulbs are an important part of the flora in many countries with a Mediterranean climate, most flowering in late winter or early spring and dying back by midsummer. Tiny and subtly marked crocuses, intensely blue grape hyacinths (*Muscari* species), brightly coloured wild tulips in reds, yellows and pinks — and many, many more — can make the early part of the year a brilliant spectacle, more than enough to make the

bulb enthusiast from cooler climes quite green with envy. Summer is less rewarding, but includes the giant wild garlics such as *Allium giganteum* and *A. christophii* with spherical heads composed of hundreds of tightly packed individual flowers. Autumn becomes colourful again as pink nerines and colchicums take advantage of the first rains.

While many herbaceous perennials do not do well in summer-drought climates, some are certainly worth considering. The elegant acanthus, for instance, are extremely vigorous, especially in slightly moister spots; the spiny eryngiums decorate dry and stony places with shapely grey leaves and blue flowers, while several species of euphorbia are excellent sources of colour early in the year. The bearded irises (including *Iris germanica*) are the best-known perennials for these places. They are able to survive extremely poor soil and prolonged drought, and their spiky leaves remain attractive outside the flowering season.

Mediterranean-climate gardeners can also cherish a handful of choice plants that only really thrive in their conditions. Examples include various members of the poppy family such as argemone, dendromecon and romneya, all with paper-thin flowers gracing grey foliage, or the various species of echium from the Canary Isles and Madeira. Particularly dramatic is the giant *Echium pininana*, which sends up immense spikes packed with thousands of individual flowers of glowing blue. Although not perennial – individual plants die after flowering – they seed themselves reliably.

Early summer sees the round head of Allium christophii *standing out from amongst the silvery evergreen foliage and mauve flowers of sage and lavender, whilst the yellow flowers of the rue bring an attractive shade of complementary colour.*

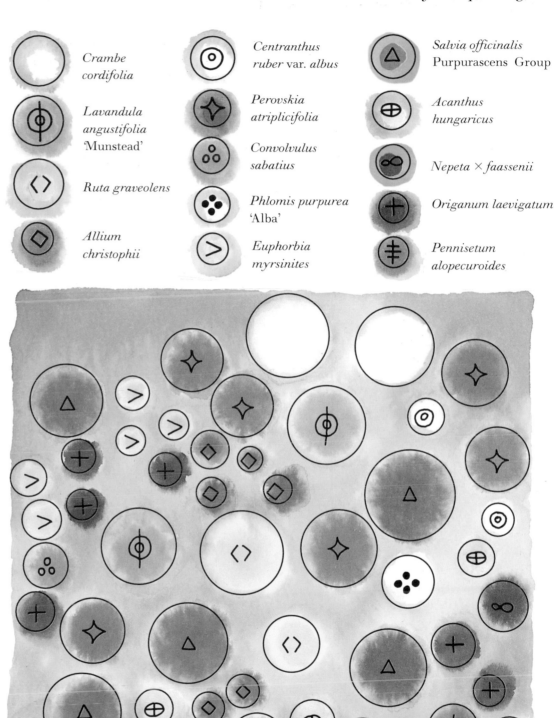

Crambe cordifolia

Lavandula angustifolia 'Munstead'

Ruta graveolens

Allium christophii

Centranthus ruber var. *albus*

Perovskia atriplicifolia

Convolvulus sabatius

Phlomis purpurea 'Alba'

Euphorbia myrsinites

Salvia officinalis Purpurascens Group

Acanthus hungaricus

Nepeta × faassenii

Origanum laevigatum

Pennisetum alopecuroides

1m
3ft

Plantings for dry areas

A silver artemisia, purple-leaved sedum and a feathery stipa grass are a reminder that foliage and form can be as important as flower colour for beauty in the garden. Plants native to dry regions often have attractive silver, grey or blue foliage, usually a result of waxy or hairy surfaces that help to protect them from drought. Many are evergreen which is an additional advantage to the gardener.

But attractive flower colour – mauve Tulbaghia violacea, *pale yellow* Anthemis tinctoria *and a deeper yellow helichrysum – also features in this planting, and on the right is the exceptionally good blue of an agapanthus.*

Steppe plantings

THE NAME 'STEPPE' IS GIVEN to the grasslands of seasonally dry parts of the Ukraine and Russia, although there are outlying pieces on sandy soils throughout central Europe. Similar is the 'shortgrass prairie' of the USA and Canada, found in a belt to the east of the Rockies. The name 'steppe' has been lent to a style of gardening that can bring colour and interest to anywhere which has a dry and/or poor soil, but which has winters too cold for many of the shrubby species that flourish in warmer climates.

Grass is the basis of the natural steppe, and some should be included in a steppe garden. The majority of other steppe and shortgrass-prairie species are herbaceous perennials, together with bulbs and a few shrubs. One immediately apparent aspect of steppes is how sparse the vegetation is, with gaps between plants. In nature this is a reflection of the paucity of moisture and sometimes of nutrients in the soil. In the garden this needs to be replicated, as most of the plants do not like to be shaded at the

base. Leaving such gaps may seem like an open invitation for opportunist annual weeds to invade, which indeed they may start to do. However, the dry soil is unsuitable for their growth and they will not cause the trouble they might on a moister site. In regions of higher summer rainfall they might become more of a problem. For such places the 'gravel garden' may be more appropriate. Here steppe and other dry-land plants are grown in soil covered with a thick blanket of coarse gravel, which greatly inhibits weed-seed germination.

The year starts with bulbs. Most of the varieties mentioned for dry area plantings are suitable, in particular the large number of dwarf tulip species, which relish being baked by the sun among thin vegetation after they have become dormant. By late spring the first perennials will be flowering, rapidly becoming a very colourful spectacle. Varieties of bearded irises can be added to contribute an extraordinary range of colours. The gardener who wants a more naturalistic or subtle spectacle can eschew the hybrids and concentrate on the original species, most of

which – like *I. germanica* – are mauve and blue, although some are strikingly striped in brown and yellow, like *I. variegata*.

Along with the irises, red and white valerian (*Centranthus ruber* and *C.r. albus*) will thrive and often self-seed, as will silvery-leaved euphorbias (such as *E. · myrsinites*) and the majestic tall flower spikes of eremurus. Gaps between the larger plants can be filled with alpine or rockery plants like dwarf campanulas (for example *C. cochleariifolia*), thymes (such as *Thymus caespitosus*) and dwarf spreading acaenas from New Zealand.

By midsummer the irises and other earlier flowers will have faded and other perennials taken their places along with the first of the

BELOW LEFT *Pink* Dictamnus albus *var.* purpureus *and magenta* Geranium sanguineum *light up a dry bank. Various alliums flower later.*

BELOW *Yellow asphodel, magenta* Gladiolus byzantinus, *purple nepeta and a pale yellow onosma form a powerful colour combination in early summer.*

grasses to flower. The tall yellow flower spikes of mulleins (*Verbascum* species) are among the easiest plants to get going, although like the valerian, they can sometimes self-seed too enthusiastically. Their strongly vertical forms offer a dramatic contrast to the predominantly low-growing habit of most steppe vegetation. Catmint (*Nepeta* × *faassenii* and related species) is a useful long-flowering low-growing perennial which consorts well with the silvery foliage of plants such as artemisias.

After midsummer the steppe will have relatively few flowers, plants in dry places needing to flower early to avoid summer drought. The rich purple flowers of origanums (closely related to the herb oregano) will be at their best and much can be made of the clear blue of *Perovskia abrotanoides*, an upright shrubby plant invaluable for this time of year. But it is the grasses that now come into their own. *Stipa gigantea* may live up to its name and grow to giant proportions, but it never dominates. Its vast sprays of flowers (and later seed-heads) lack solidity, making them effectively transparent, half-revealing whatever lies behind through a haze of straw-coloured flower and stem.

Smaller stipas are without exception worth growing, especially *S. pennata* with its immensely long feathery awns which blow in the breeze. Completely different in shape and effect are the pennisetums, grasses which form low and compact clumps, by late summer a mass of soft flower that combines beautifully with nepetas and origanums. Many of the best dry-land grasses are blue or silver-grey. *Festuca glauca* forms a low, compact clump, while *Helictotrichon sempervirens* is similar in habit but larger. Where space permits, species of elymus produce leaves of steely-blue from a spreading rootstock.

ABOVE *A dry steppe habitat in early summer is arguably one of the most colourful garden sights. After the irises are over, a variety of other interplanted perennials and grasses will start to perform.*

BELOW *The blue of flax* (Linum perenne) *is a lovely complement to the bright yellow of St John's wort* (Hypericum) *which, along with thrift* (Armeria maritima) *covers an area of stony ground.*

Coastal plantings

Plants that grow by the sea have to endure the winter storms, salt spray and intense summer sun all year round, as well as the poor soils that are all too common. To deal with these harsh climatic conditions many coastal plants have evolved protective devices such as waxy-textured grey leaves to reduce water loss and salt damage — incidentally making themselves very attractive in the process. Plant species from similarly stressful environments such as semi-desert areas and windy moorlands will often thrive along the coast alongside the maritime plants. Good plants for the coast can usually be spotted easily by their leathery or waxy leaves, which are often grey or blue.

Planting in dunes

In addition to harsh climatic conditions, coastal plants frequently have to cope with dry and nutrient-poor sandy or shingly soils, often unstable ones as in dunes. If you are faced with sand that needs stabilizing then binding it together is a priority. Certain ornamental grasses with running roots, like sea oats (*Uniola paniculata*) and beach panic grass (*Panicum amarum*) will do this, along with the highly effective but rather dull marram grass (*Ammophila arenaria*). Once stabilized, dunes can be made home to some very attractive plant communities.

As well as these specialist grasses, there are many others that do well at the coast. Northern sea oats (*Chasmanthium*

Red roses and pale yellow Californian poppies (Eschscholzia californica) *bring colour to this seaside planting. The mild climate of many coastal areas also allows exotic flora such as giant echiums (rear left) to flourish.*

latifolium) is a particularly distinctive one, with very distinctive large seed heads. Switchgrass (*Panicum virgatum*), a prairie species by nature, usually thrives, and is particularly valuable in the autumn, turning the kind of rich colours we normally expect from trees.

Thistly eryngiums will be at home; in fact the rather fetching sea holly (*Eryngium maritimum*) is difficult to grow anywhere else. Softer in appearance are the evening primroses (*Oenothera* species), which self-seed easily in sandy soil – just as well, as plants tend to be short-lived. Several members of the mallow family are shore-dwellers, from *Lavatera maritima*, which can grow within a few metres of the high-tide mark, to marsh mallow (*Althaea officinalis*) and *Kosteletzkya virginica*, both of which grow well in the poorly drained patches frequently found among dunes. Plants with large flowers such as these and the evening primroses can be contrasted with silvery foliage and with species with flower heads composed of masses of tiny flowers. Sea lavender (*Limonium* species – no relation to true lavender) is useful in this respect, as is the extraordinary sea kale (*Crambe maritima*), which makes a clump of large dark green leaves, from which a vast head of cream flowers springs in early summer. This, too, is one of the limited number of plants that can grow just above the shoreline.

The area just inland from the sea itself is particularly testing, often being directly splashed by sea spray. In addition to those plants mentioned, there is the sea pea (*Lathyrus japonicus*) and, for very stony places, thrift (*Armeria maritima*). The ability of the latter to insinuate its tight cushions into cracks in rocks (and into garden walls) where there is no soil to speak of is quite remarkable.

Coastal gardening entails a major element of the experimental. Little is written about the subject, so gardeners have few sources of guidance. There may be plenty of wild flowers that grow by the sea, but they are often unavailable commercially, sometimes because – as in the case of sea holly – what grows easily by the coast seems to sulk inland. Keen gardeners need to collect a few seeds from attractive plants whenever they see them (see pages 120-21). In addition, they need to be prepared to use trial and error, planting species from other dry habitats and seeing which flourish and which do not. Once you have found something that does well, try other members of its genus.

Climate and wind

One major advantage that the seaside gardener enjoys is the relative mildness of the climate at the coast. Frosts are both less frequent and less severe than those inland, allowing a wider range of slightly tender plants to be grown, including many from Mediterranean climates. Wind may be a major problem, but not necessarily so. Oceanic gales may be capable of a lot of structural damage but they are not generally cold and many tough-leaved but not very hardy plants will cope with them. Bitterly cold winter winds can of course severely limit plant selection. However, they are often dry and reduce winter rainfall, and some seemingly tender plants will happily grow in places dominated by them, because they can cope with cold alone much better than cold and wet together. Get to know your prevailing winds and plant or erect windbreaks to soften their impact.

Plants from Mediterranean climates, such as lavenders, or from dry habitats, such as the Stipa *grasses and tall yellow mulleins here, often flourish at the coast since they tend to be resistant to drying winds.*

Techniques

By selecting plants that will thrive naturally in given conditions, we are spared much of the time-consuming and costly 'soil improvement' that is so much a part of traditional gardening. Nevertheless, site preparation is vital, especially if seed is to be sown. The most important task is to remove weeds and weed seed.

When the site has been prepared, seeds can be sown and plants put in. Both will need close care and attention for the first year, as young plants are very vulnerable. Once this initial phase is over, progressively less attention is needed as the planting matures. After two to three years maintenance will be greatly reduced. However, skilled and timely intervention will always be needed to maintain an environment that is not only attractive but rich in species.

The new perennial garden often requires large numbers of plants, making a knowledge of propagation vital. Fortunately many are easy to multiply using division and will grow rapidly once replanted. This is Geranium *'Claridge Druce', one of the finest and most useful perennials for suppressing weeds in difficult places.*

Meadows: planning for action

If you are faced with an area of existing garden such as lawn or a conventional border that you wish to replant, or alternatively rough grass and other unattractive weedy species, it is a relatively simple matter to remove what is already there and to start afresh. If, however, you are faced by a semi-natural area, such as an old field or woodland, where there is a mixture of desirable wildflowers and grasses and perhaps a few perennial weeds, you need to choose whether to clear and start afresh or to improve the existing flora by selective weeding and planting. Shaded areas and poor soils, where vegetation is relatively sparse, are fairly easy to 'enhance'. Turning rough grass into a wildflower meadow is more problematic, yet if there are any attractive, interesting or uncommon species present then this should be seriously considered.

How an area of grass is enhanced to become a colourful meadow depends upon the final desired look. A reasonably fertile soil is best planted with robust perennials and prairie plants, which can compete successfully with grasses (as described on pages 76-7). If the ground appears less fertile – perhaps because some existing smaller wildflowers are already present – then it is worth considering trying to manage it so as to encourage these less vigorous wildflowers to increase and spread.

Camassias, clover and buttercups grow in profusion and will thrive in a meadow on a damp soil. The ox-eye daisy is short-lived and will not persist for more than a few years. Camassias should be introduced to the meadow as bulbs.

This can be done by mowing at appropriate times and removing the clippings. Over a period of a few years this regime will considerably lower the nutrient level of the soil, making it less suitable for competitive grasses and weeds and allowing more colourful plants to thrive. More species can be introduced as plugs (see pages 112-3) or as mature plants (see pages 118-9).

The fact that many of the most attractive and diverse wildflower communities are to be found on poor, thin soils where large grasses do not flourish means that, to create a successful meadow planting comprising such species, the soil's fertility must be reduced. This is the complete opposite of what gardeners have traditionally done. Stripping off the top layer of topsoil is one rather drastic but proven way of removing most of the soil nutrient. It is arguably a major intervention in the environment, but may be justified on the grounds that doing so provides better conditions for the majority of native plants, including many of the less common species. It also minimizes the likelihood that the meadow will be swamped by the results of human interference in the environment in the form of agricultural rye grass and farm weeds like docks.

Wildflowers of thin soils, or dry-land and steppe species, will flourish on crushed builders' rubble and – more attractively – on gravel. If you are stuck with piles of rubble, always expensive to move away, you can use them to provide a suitable home for a good variety of these species. Soils that you know to be full of weed seed could actually be covered in such material, effectively burying the seed bank and providing a suitable habitat for colourful lime-loving wildflowers to flourish unhindered. During summer there will be enough vegetation to cover the rubble, although areas might be unattractively exposed during the winter.

Choose drought-tolerant silver and grey-leaved evergreens to provide some year-round cover.

Human activity often results in the creation of a rich weed seed bank. All those weed seeds that lie dormant in the soil for many years are waiting for the right opportunity, light and air to pounce on the unsuspecting gardener. Earth that has been disturbed in the last ten years is especially problematic. Simply exposing fresh soil during the growing season will rapidly show how rich the seed bank is: if a large number of weeds germinate then you may have to resign yourself to systematically destroying it before planting. Continually hoeing off all the germinating seedlings will greatly reduce it in the top five centimetres (two inches), but it may take a whole season. Wildflower seed may then be sown with a reasonable chance of success, if the soil is not disturbed below this depth. Planting, which involves greater soil disturbance, will bring up the seed from deeper layers. Mulching around new plantings, which can dramatically reduce weed seed growth, is probably the best approach in such circumstances.

Preparing the soil

Soil for sowing need not – and should not – be deeply dug, especially where there is a danger of bringing up buried weed seed, but must be finely broken up on the surface to allow the tiny seedling roots to enter the soil as easily as possible. Raking, to separate out and then break up larger lumps of soil, is the most effective way to create this fine tilth on most soils. Heavy soils are best dug over in autumn and left for winter's frosts to break them up and make a difficult task slightly lighter. If it seems impossible to create a sufficiently decent tilth for seed sowing, then consider planting plugs (see pages 112-3) as an alternative.

Meadows: sowing direct

Planting an entire meadow with plants bought in from nurseries is something that almost everyone but the most wealthy and impatient will balk at. Sowing from seed is much cheaper, although it can be problematic – nothing like as easy as the sales blurb on the side of a colourful seed packet or a 'meadow in a can' tries to make us believe. Creating a meadow involves not just preparing the site and sowing, but several years of skilled aftercare before it becomes a viable and reasonably stable plant community, a truly low-maintenance, mow-once-a-year habitat.

Sowing a whole planting is most practical for wildflower meadows of locally native species. Sowing a mixture of grasses, wildflowers and introduced or garden

perennials is theoretically possible, but prohibitively expensive except on a very small scale (and small meadows are not the most successful visually). The exception is if you are able to collect enough seed of your own – from plants already in the garden, or from friends and neighbours – to be able to supply the greater part of your needs. It is generally meadows and prairies that are sown, but there are also seed mixtures available for semi-shaded and wetland areas. Seed mixes are not a practical proposition for shade, as most shade-loving plants spread primarily vegetatively in the short term; compared with sun-loving plants, they tend to set little seed and to develop slowly. It is interesting that most stress-tolerant plants are not great setters of seed, and dry-land plants (other than annuals, which are really stress avoiders rather than true stress tolerators) produce little seed either.

The fact that sowing effectively restricts us to using locally native wildflowers does not,

of course, limit us to having only these in the meadow. A small number of other non-native perennials can be planted at the same time as the seed is sown (see pages 112-3) or once the meadow is established (pages 118-9).

Sowing is best carried out at a time of year when there is likely to be as long a season of adequate moisture ahead as possible, and a minimum of harsh weather. In hot summer/cool winter climates, autumn or early winter, after the first rains, is the only sensible time to sow; this timing allows growth through the winter so that the young plants can face the summer drought

Sowing in furrows enables you to differentiate between seedlings that you have sown and weed seedlings, since anything that comes up outside a furrow will be a weed. Make furrows, up to 1 cm/⅜ in deep with a trowel or rake (below left), sow the seed in the furrow (centre) and then fill in with a rake (right).

ahead with their roots well established in the soil. In maritime climates with capriciously unreliable winters, either autumn or spring is possible. Autumn sowing can result in better plant establishment and better germination of species that need cold to come up (see pages 122-3), but a particularly cold winter may kill some of them. Spring sowing avoids the risk of a hard winter but opens up the greater possibility of seedlings not being robust enough to withstand a dry spell. Gardens in continental climates – with cold winters and hot summers – have the smallest window of opportunity. Sowing can be done only in spring. Quite apart from the dangers of winter, many plants native to such areas need fairly high temperatures to germinate. Some irrigation to help through the first summer may well be necessary.

Whatever the climate, sowing should be done on a windless day, on to moist soil, preferably with rain forecast. The rate for most grass/wildflower mixtures is 3-5 g per square metre/(about 1/8 oz per square yard); for flower seed only, sow 1-2 g per square metre/(around 1/20 oz per square yard). Handling such minute quantities of seed is almost impossible, so many people mix the seed thoroughly with a suitable weight of sand. Small patches of ground can be broadcast-sown by hand. Sow larger areas with a commercial seed/fertilizer spreader. Whichever way you choose, it can be helpful to mark the plot out into sections and divide up the seed (or seed plus sand) into an allocation per section to allow for fair distribution; there is nothing worse than getting halfway across before realizing that you have been too generous with the first half and the packet is practically empty for the rest. It is also very difficult to sow evenly, so the best method is to halve the quantity of seed for each section and sow twice, once going (for example) north-south and then a second time from east to west. Save a little seed to resow unsuccessful areas should this be necessary.

After sowing, a gentle raking is advisable to bury a proportion of the seed and ensure good contact with the soil.

If you have some species available as separate amounts, it is possible to create drifts of particular plants for either ecological or aesthetic reasons, sowing a concentration of meadowsweet (*Filipendula ulmaria*) in a moister area, for example, or creating a splash of violet and yellow in one particular area with a concentration of ironweed (*Vernonia* species) and goldenrod (*Solidago*). Remember, though, to blur the boundaries for the natural look.

A wildflower meadow will take a year or two to become the colourful spectacle you desire, and many more to become a stable plant community. Annuals can be used to provide a temporary splash of colour in the first year, and often enough of them will self-sow to keep the odd one coming up for a few more. An added advantage of using annuals is that they act as a 'nurse crop' for the more slow-growing perennial wildflowers and grasses, shading them while they are seedlings.

Broadcast sowing is difficult to do evenly so it is best to go over the ground twice, from different directions. Allow the seed to dribble out of the front of a loosely clenched fist while your hand describes a figure of eight (top). *It may be an idea to practise this action first with some sand. Raking over afterwards is important to get good contact between the soil and the seed* (middle). *Only a year after sowing the meadow can be almost covered with plants* (bottom).

Meadows: seed mixtures

Choosing a seed mixture that is appropriate to the ecology of the site, whether it is wet or dry, clay, limestone or sand, is important for the eventual success of the planting. A careful reading of the ingredients is advisable, too, particularly to check that any grass species included are not strong-growing types, such as false oat grass (*Arrhenatherum elatius*), creeping soft grass (*Holcus mollis*) or rye grass (*Lolium perenne*). In most areas you can usually find several suppliers, and since meadow mixes often differ markedly in composition, origin of seed and price, it is wise to shop around.

Besides noting the grass composition of the mix, it is also worth looking out for certain other vigorous plants that you might not want. Yarrow (*Achillea millefolium*), ox-eye daisy (*Leucanthemum vulgare*) and wild carrot (*Daucus carota*) are all very quick to establish, but can grow so vigorously that they hamper the development of other plants. They are frequently included in North American seed mixes, although they are introduced plants, not true natives. Many North American mixes also contain a large proportion of colourful annuals at the expense of reliably perennial plants.

Choosing a seed mix composed of locally grown seed can also be important. Seed imported from another region, even if it is the same species, might be genetically different and not so well adapted to your local climatic conditions.

Seed mixes are usually sold as approximately three parts grass to one part wildflower. You also have the option of buying only the wildflower seed, and no grasses. This may seem a lot more expensive, but the seed will be sown more thinly than a grass-and-flower mix. You could use it for a relatively small area where strong colours are needed or for sowing into grass. Some growers actually recommend using this as the basis for large-scale plantings, allowing nature to manage the introduction of grasses through spontaneous arrivals. The danger of such an approach is that perennials by themselves do not provide the ground coverage that grasses do, allowing weed seedlings to insinuate themselves. Such sowings would probably work best on very infertile soils in areas where there is little weed seed on the wind.

You can make your own seed mix, tailored to suit the ecology of your garden, personal preference or a colour scheme – a meadow of pink, purple and blue flowers, for instance. Bulk seed suppliers usually state in their catalogues the weight of seed needed to raise so many plants, so you can work out how much to get of each kind. Some species will be limited by cost, others by the fact that if they are vigorous you may want to restrict their numbers.

Establishing meadows

The magic of germination will happen quite quickly, with grasses and members of the daisy family in the lead. Some species – those with complex germination requirements (see pages 142-3) – may not appear until after a year or so. Once the young plants have got to a height of around 7 cm/3 in, they should be mown to around 4 cm/1 ½ in. This will limit the growth of the more vigorous grasses and perennials and also of many weeds, giving the slower and often more desirable plants a chance. Thereafter the young meadow should be mown whenever it gets to the 7 cm/3 in mark, though if an initial nurse crop of annuals is grown, then cutting should be left until the autumn. Clippings should always be removed.

Combining sowing with planting

There is no reason why planting should not be combined with sowing, except that it interferes with the mowing during the establishment phase described above. In situations where it is known that there will be a weed problem, frequent mowing will be needed as a control measure for weeds. Sowings of more vigorous wildflowers, particularly prairie or wetland species, may be more practicable.

Seed can also be sown into existing turf, although it has to be said that because of the competition from established plants, it is often not successful. However, it happens all the time in nature, as seed of new species blows in on the wind, so is well worth persisting, so long as you are prepared for disappointments. Grass, such as an existing lawn, should be 'scarified' or scratched hard with a rake to pull out dead material and leave lines or patches of bare earth. Seed of wildflowers may be sown into these bare patches and covered with sieved soil or raked over again to cover.

An alternative – and somewhat more reliable – method is to plant 'plugs' or seedlings into turf (see pages 112-3).

A mixture of perennial, annual and biennial seeds can make a colourful meadow. Poppies are an annual that often self-seed for a few years after they have been sown. Ox-eye daisies are a short-lived but vigorous perennial and blue Campanula patula *is a biennial that will only persist on sites that receive some soil disturbance every few years, for example scarifying with a rake.*

Meadows: combining sowing and planting

Sowing a meadow is a risky business, putting you at the mercy of the weather, soil conditions, weed growth, birds and other seed-eating animals. It is also quite expensive if done on a large scale, which may be an argument for doing a big area a bit at a time, learning and gaining experience as you go. As a halfway stage between sowing and planting, there are various other techniques that reduce the risk factor. They are particularly useful for places where there are problems with sowing seed, where a lot of annual weeds are present or where the soil is very heavy and impossible to break down into a suitable tilth.

Wildflower turf

Wildflower turf is much like ordinary turf, except that it consists of a mixture of both young grasses and wildflowers. It can be bought from specialist nurseries or, more cheaply, grown yourself. Whereas ordinary lawn turf is laid out to meet up with no gaps, individual pieces of wildflower turf are placed leaving gaps of soil about 30 cm/ 12 in between them. The grasses, followed by the perennials, will gradually grow out

Sowing combined with planting allows you to combine a matrix of species available as seed with other, more select varieties best grown or only available as single plants. The larger plants will also help to give an 'instant' effect to the scheme. First place the plants where you want them to grow, then plant them firmly (right). *Broadcast the seed evenly over the prepared ground* (middle right), *then rake it in carefully around the plants* (far right).

from the patches of turf and meet up over the course of a growing season.

It is possible to make your own wild-flower turf by sowing a seed mix onto a seed bed. Since this seed bed is going to be considerably smaller than the meadow (one square metre or square yard of turf will cover about four times that area), it is possible and desirable to prepare it to a very high standard. Forking and raking will produce a nice tilth. If annual weeds are a problem, you could sterilize the area using a flame gun. If your soil is so heavy or full of weed seeds that even this is not possible, then it could be worthwhile buying in some selected topsoil to use as a seed bed, creating a layer a minimum of 8-10 cm/3-4 in deep as topping over your existing soil.

The turf will probably be ready a few months after sowing. Since most wildflowers have deeper roots than grasses, the turf has to be used without too much delay, other-wise lifting it will fatally damage a large number of the plants. When it is ready, cut it up and distribute the turves over the area chosen for the meadow. Needless to say, the

site should be well weeded and prepared. Loosen the soil beneath the turves and plant them flush with the surface.

Using plugs

Growing wildflowers in plugs is perhaps the easiest way to obtain large numbers of plants from a meadow mix for planting out. Plugs are small chunks of compost containing one or more plants (more in our illustration), each usually no more than 2.5 cm/1in across. Commercial growers raise thousands of bedding plants, vegetable seedlings and garden perennials in plug trays of between several dozen and several hundred cells. They then discard the empty trays, so you may find it possible to beg or scavenge as many as you need. Trays in which the cells are larger than 1.7 cm/⅝ in are the most useful for our needs; below this size the plugs produced tend to be too small to survive in less-than-perfect conditions.

A meadow mix can be thinly sown over plug trays filled with a conventional seed-sowing or pot-plant compost, at the rate of a few seeds per cell. A thin layer of compost is

used to cover them and they are kept watered in a cool place until they germinate. Once the seedlings are showing plenty of root at the bottom they are ready for planting out, although if necessary they can be kept much longer in their trays (see page 126). Space them at 10-20 cm/4-8 in intervals when planting out.

Using plugs is not only a great advantage on heavy soils, or anywhere else where sowing might be difficult, but it also enables you to use seed more economically. It allows you to prepare and plant out a mixture of both meadow-mix plugs and young plants grown in plugs from expensive garden perennial seed. These are best produced more conventionally with one seedling per plug. Since the grasses, wildflowers and other perennials will all be going in at the same time, at the same stage of life, it will be easier to care for them all together.

Once either wildflower turves or plugs have been planted out and allowed to grow on they can be mown, much as a more conventionally sown meadow would be. But beware: they must be well rooted in. The

action of a mower or strimmer is quite capable of pulling them out of the ground if rooting is only superficial. You can also plant individual perennials directly into the ground and then broadcast-sow grass seed or meadow mix around them on the prepared ground. This is particularly useful if you want to include perennial varieties that are usually only available as single plants, or where the specimens are best grown singly from seed – that is, initially without competition. Planting and then sowing gives the favoured perennials a head start, and when they grow they will make the planting scheme look more established.

Plugs of wildflower meadow mix are a highly effective way of planting smaller areas. Sow the meadow mix in plug trays and when the individual plugs have made good growth (top right), *plant them out at regular intervals up to 20 cm/8 in apart* (right). *Results are encouragingly rapid, and weeds are easy to remove between the plugs.*

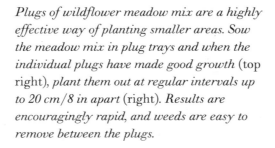

Tackling weeds

A WEED CAN BE DEFINED as 'a plant in the wrong place'. What is quite desirable in one context (an attractive but strongly spreading plant in a large garden) is unsuitable in another (the same plant in a very small garden). Species that spread rapidly at the expense of desired plants are usually classed as weeds, although in the context of the naturally inspired garden we may allow certain exceptions. Dandelions, for example, are extremely colourful and might be acceptable if they do not threaten too many other species. Stinging nettles are unattractive and invasive, but are one of the best food sources for butterfly caterpillars, and so may be permitted to grow in an out-of-the-way corner.

The critic may say that the wilder versions of the new perennial garden – perennials growing in rough grass, for instance, or a meadow of wildflowers – are 'weedy' or 'weed-ridden'. While what one regards as tidy or untidy is all a matter of personal taste, there is no denying that a few weeds are much less noticeable in a wild garden context than in a conventional border.

There are basically two ways in which the presence of weeds can threaten new plantings. One is when strongly competitive perennials that spread by underground roots – such as nettles, ground elder, bindweed or couch grass – are present. These are capable of regenerating from tiny pieces of broken root left in the soil. Perennials with deep tap roots, like dandelions and docks, will also sprout again if only their top is removed. The second menace comes in the form of weed seeds. Some of these are from perennials like dandelions and thistles; others are from disturbance-tolerant annuals that spring up from bare or disturbed earth, to flower and seed again in the time it takes to go away on holiday and return. Once scattered, buried seed may remain viable for many years. Annual weed seedlings are a problem only in new plantings, before they are rapidly displaced by strong-growing established perennials and grasses. They can, however, make sowing a wildflower meadow from seed practically impossible.

Root-spreading perennial weeds are probably our greatest enemy. They can overwhelm all but the most vigorous plants, bringing our efforts to nought. In grass, you can weaken and eventually remove them by repeated mowing, but in a planting based on other perennials they need to be removed at the outset. There are various ways you can try to eliminate weeds:

Hand-digging
Practicable only on the smallest scale, this is laborious, and not terribly effective – as little pieces of perennial weed root always remain. This technique also does nothing to eradicate weed seeds.

Black plastic
Covering ground with black plastic during a growing season before planting starves perennial weeds of light so that they die. This is a remarkably effective method with most weeds (apart from horsetail). It does nothing about the seed bank, however.

Ensure that the plastic does not blow away, that the edges are buried and that any weed emerging through holes or cracks is dealt with. Used black plastic should be burnt, not thrown away; it creates hardly any smoke, whereas plastic in landfill sites will still be there in a thousand years.

Remove all unwanted vegetation before sowing or planting. Here a glyphosate-based weedkiller has been used to kill the vegetation (left). *Rotovate the ground* (middle) *and then rake off the dead turf and weeds* (right).

Animals

Animals are only an option for the larger country garden! Pigs will grub out buried roots with remarkable efficiency, while hens will do the same for seeds. Their manure will increase fertility, which may or may not be desirable.

Hoeing

Constantly hoeing off and/or rotovating the top few centimetres of soil over the course of a growing season, as and when new growth appears, will pretty well exhaust the seed bank, thereby eliminating the worst of the annual weed problem. Perennial weeds will be weakened, but some may survive. Where an area is to be sown, for a wildflower meadow for instance, this kind of shallow cultivation is all that is needed.

Weedkillers

Not everyone finds chemicals acceptable, but I certainly recommend some of the specific systemic weedkillers for perennials. They work by being absorbed by the leaves and taken down to the roots, killing the entire plant. One of the most effective is glyphosate. It is of very low toxicity and is rapidly broken down by bacteria in the soil. Grasses and docks are very susceptible, but some weeds such as ground elder and nettles are not seriously affected. For these, seek local suppliers' advice on what other weedkillers are suitable. For tough, woody-stemmed plants – brambles included – I recommend the extremely safe, if expensive, ammonium sulphamate, which also breaks down rapidly in the soil.

Flame gun

An infestation of annual weeds can be killed by scorching the top few centimetres of soil with a flame gun. This is useful to clear a small area such as a seed bed.

ABOVE *Dandelions are a good example of a plant that is beautiful but too vigorous in a small garden, where they make it difficult for other wildflowers to grow with them. If you have enough space, an expanse of dandelions can look stunning.*

BELOW *Precision weedkilling can be done with a brush and a mixture of weedkiller and wallpaper paste that eliminates dripping* (left), *or with a hand-held sprayer and a cowl cut from the top of an old plastic bottle to prevent the spray drifting* (right).

Preparing for planting

Planting the new perennial garden is in some ways the same as planting the conventional garden. Actually choosing the places where plants are to go is somewhat different, however; our aim is to distribute plants in an artistic but natural-looking arrangement, as if they appeared there by themselves. The most unconventional plantings of all are meadow gardens, where either locally native plants or a mixture of local wildflowers and introduced species blend together in a grass matrix. Growing such meadows from seed gives the gardener little control over the placing of individual plants and leaves more to the whims of nature. If you are going to base your planting on home-grown or bought-in plants, however, you have to decide not only where but when to do the planting.

The basic choice is between spring and autumn, although the garden centre and ubiquitous pot-grown plant enable today's gardeners to plant at whatever time of year they fancy. Most people get enthusiastic about gardening in spring, rushing out to plant and sow on the first sunny day after winter. Traditionally planting was done in autumn, in the days when plants were almost invariably dug up from the open ground and despatched by mail order. The old ways were more in tune with nature, and autumn planting is best for the vast majority of hardy plants, at least in climates which do not have severe winters with constant sub-zero temperatures. The reason is that many plants, while dormant above ground, remain busily growing roots through the winter months, establishing themselves securely before sending out leaves in spring and having to endure the heat and potential drought of summer. It is obvious that in climates with hot summers and cool, moist winters, autumn planting is vital for survival through the first season.

In maritime climates, where summers are unpredictable and often wet, it is theoretically possible to plant at any time of year, but this can be a risk in summer, unless water is to hand for irrigation, so autumn is still wisest. The only exception to the wisdom of autumn planting is in climates with consistently very cold winters, where there is no chance of growth during the winter and the additional risk of the frost heaving young plants out of the ground at that time.

Plants are often bought in containers these days, and the almost complete lack of root disturbance involved in planting from a pot means that spring or even early summer planting is more of a possibility than in the days when everything was sold bare-rooted. Digging up a plant for transplanting bare-rooted destroys the fine roots necessary for the uptake of water, making the plant much more vulnerable to drying out. However, there are points in favour of the old ways. Herbaceous plants almost invariably achieve a much bigger size in the ground than when grown in pots and are often considerably cheaper to buy. The greater size of a bare-rooted plant may allow it to establish and make an impressive specimen more quickly than a pot-grown one, at least if planted in autumn or winter.

Soil for planting needs to be deeply dug, to allow plant roots to penetrate as deeply as possible, bringing them into contact with moisture reserves deep down, often essential

Yellow day lilies, purple erigerons and pennisetum grasses flowering in midsummer are interplanted, but in discrete groups for maximum impact.

for survival in the first year. It is possible, although pretty demanding physically, to double-dig a whole small area, as vegetable gardeners do. For larger areas, or heavy or stony soils, this is unrealistic. It is better to concentrate on deep-digging in specific places where you are going to put plants, especially expensive or important ones.

Conventional wisdom dictates the digging in of water-retentive compost and a source of nutrients (bonemeal has always been a favourite) when planting. Research indicates that this is unnecessary and may even be counterproductive; compost or peat can hold so much water that it encourages decay, while it is suggested that too many nutrients in the vicinity of the roots discourages them from growing to seek more. The exceptions come when you are faced with 'difficult ground' that does need improving – (see pages 118-9).

Before you begin to put plants in, they can be laid out in position while you make the final adjustments to your plan. You can easily move around plants in containers. In winter, provided the weather is cool and wet, it is also possible to leave bare-rooted plants on the soil surface for several days without harm, allowing you to make decisions, marshall everything you need and dig the holes for your key plants.

The concept of plant sociability discussed on pages 38-9 gives a good idea of how to decide which plants to group together and which to space farther apart.

1) Architectural perennials in the form of the grasses *Miscanthus sinensis* and *Molinia caerulea* 'Moorhexe' (sociability I) dominate part of an open border in late summer: their positions were the first to be determined. Between them three varieties of low-sociability monarda are scattered through low clumps of medium-sociability *Geranium* × *magnificum* and *G. endressii*, which had

their main flowering season in summer. Earlier still, *Aquilegia vulgaris* (low sociability) and bergenias (medium sociability) provided interest.

2) In a meadow, wildflowers tend to be very scattered, but with some species concentrated in certain areas in drifts, always blending with their neighbours. Here a drift of *Filipendula ulmaria* meets a drift of *Succisa pratensis*. Sowing seed to capture the essence of these ebbs and flows of plant populations is the artistic key to making a successful wildflower meadow.

3) Woodland plants in nature are often low-growing and occur in clumps, as they tend to reproduce by spreading vegetatively

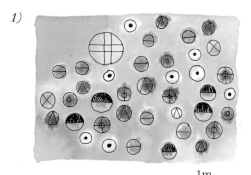

1)

⊞	*Miscanthus sinensis*
⊗	*Molinia caerulea* 'Moorhexe'
⊘	*Aquilegia vulgaris*
⊖	*Geranium* × *magnificum*
⊖	*Geranium endressi*
⊙	*Bergenia* 'Silberlicht'
◎	*Monarda* 'Chippewa'
⊕	*Monarda* 'Comanche'
⊕	*Monarda* 'Squaw'

1m / 3ft

rather than by seed. They are thus quite 'sociable' plants and need to be grown in groups to achieve impact, like the carpeting *Galium odoratum* and *Ajuga reptans* and the clump-forming pulmonaria here. Taller woodland-ers such as the single stems of *Campanula trachelium* (which tends to spread by seed) are found as populations of more scattered individuals, although in the garden some loose grouping shows them off to best advantage. Prepare individual planting holes with added leaf-mould to give plants a good start.

2)

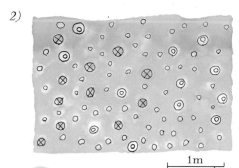

1m / 3ft

○	Grass species
◎	*Filipendula ulmaria*
⊗	*Succisa pratensis*

3)

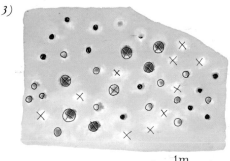

1m / 3ft

×	*Campanula trachelium*
⊗	*Pulmonaria rubra*
○	*Galium odoratum*
•	*Ajuga reptans*

Planting in special conditions

WHILE WE ARE AIMING TO GROW plants that thrive in the given conditions and have seen how even seemingly unpromising terrain such as piles of rubble and waterlogged clay can bring forth a multitude of colourful flowers, we may have spots where we feel we must undertake some soil improvement. Plant communities have adapted over millions of years to make the most of an enormous range of habitats, but human activity has created yet others, often deeply inhospitable to plants. Man-made soil damage can be one of the most problematic areas for the gardener.

People with small urban plots nearly always have to garden around buildings, where the ground may be compacted, the soil full of rubble, and topsoil perhaps totally absent. If such a site is well-drained and has a sunny aspect, it may support an exciting flora of dry-land plants that relish poor soil. However, such plants will not thrive if the site is in shade, and woodland plants have a great need for moisture-retentive, humus-rich soil. This is an instance where it is worth filling planting holes with quantities of leaf-mould or similar organic material to 'improve' the dry soil for these shade-lovers. Where the site is not well drained, it may – apart from poor soil quality – be ideal for a more lush flora. Such cases may justify some expenditure of effort and money.

Deep or double digging may be necessary to open up a compacted subsoil, improve drainage and allow plant roots to penetrate more deeply. Such an exercise is also an opportunity to remove rubbish, from the almost proverbial discarded bedsteads to today's more likely reels of wire and old paint cans. There is little point in being too

assiduous, though; it is not necessary to remove all stones (or similar mineral material like broken tiles and lumps of concrete). So long as the surrounding soil is in reasonably good shape, no plant is going to mind a few lumps of rock – it is only the vegetable gardener (or the traditional bedding-plant enthusiast) whose annual digging is encumbered by stones, who needs to remove them.

Improving the soil

Incorporating material to feed the soil, to improve its ability to hold moisture and nutrients and to ensure drainage is a major part of conventional gardening practice that may be relevant on difficult or damaged soils. Adding peat is out of the question; it is greatly overrated as a material anyway, and its extraction causes major environmental damage. Well-composted bark is a waste product from forestry that is widely available and excellent for these purposes. Bought bagged, it can be expensive, but shopping around sawmills may reveal sources of cheaper bulk supplies. It does need to be well decayed before use, however. Fresh material not only contains toxins present in conifer bark but also robs soil of nitrogen as it decays. The availability of other suitable materials, from spent hops to used mushroom compost, is dependent largely on what local agriculture and industry can offer.

The opposite – and for many gardeners paradoxical – case is when the site is *too* fertile, and a much more extensive flora, with a wider range of both native and attractive plants, could be sustained if the soil was poorer. Some measures for reducing soil fertility are discussed on page 107.

Shade-loving and woodland plants may be adapted to growing in apparently poor conditions underneath trees, but this is no excuse to skimp care and effort on planting.

Tree roots may physically get in the way of digging a planting hole, and their proximity can mean local shortages of nutrients and moisture. Take some time to find suitable planting sites for your plants, and position only species known to be very tough and tolerant around the bases of the trees themselves. Dig in soil improvers such as home-made compost, leaf-mould or rotted bark when preparing planting holes for woodlanders.

Planting in grass

When creating a flowering meadow, combining garden perennials and wildflowers with established grasses (see pages 80-81), the priority is to reduce competition from the grass to give the flowers a chance to establish themselves. A circle of turf about 30-40 cm/12-16 in across should be cut and removed. (It will take with it not only the grass but incidentally most of the weed seed bank.) Dig a planting hole and plant your perennial in the centre. Keep it well watered through dry spells until it is established. Lay a mulch – of composted bark or dead turves, for example – around the plant to reduce moisture loss and prevent weed seed germination. At the end of the first year and throughout the second some maintenance will be needed to remove encroaching grass. After this, the perennials should be well enough established to cope with grass competition.

To plant in grass, you can first treat areas with a glyphosate weedkiller (top left). *Dig out circles of turf and soil* (top right) *and plant a perennial in the hole* (middle left), *carefully firming it in* (middle right). *Replace the dead turf around the plant* (bottom left) *if you know that the soil has a large weed bank. The end result* (bottom right) *can be this day lily,* Hemerocallis *'Golden Chimes', naturalized in long grass.*

Seed collection and storage

Propagating from seed is the most natural means of building up plant stocks and should be done wherever possible. One advantage of growing from seed is that it always ensures some natural variation in the resulting plants, both in looks and in their ability to survive stressful conditions. Yet growing plants from seed is not always practicable. Most shade and dry-land plants set little seed, and bulk quantities of seed of many introduced perennial species is unavailable or expensive. In these cases reproducing plants by cuttings and division is the best way of obtaining large numbers of individual specimens (see pages 124-5).

Collecting wildflower seeds

Seed may be collected from plants that you already have, from friends' gardens, or from the wild. Wild collecting needs to be done responsibly, but since wildflowers usually produce vastly more seed than ever actually grows, a limited amount of collecting will do no harm to natural populations. Seed should never be taken from plants you know to be rare, are legally protected, appear to have a localized distribution or which set very little seed. Avoid collecting, too, when plants seem to be having a bad year (as when there is a fat grub inside almost every seed pod).

Collecting seed is immensely satisfying but can also be very frustrating. Seed is designed for easy and wide dispersal, not neat collection, so finding empty pods and bare seed heads is an all-too-common experience. Seed is generally ripe when it is brown or black rather than green. Ripe seed is relatively easy to remove from its container, just as ripe apples are easy to pick, whereas unripe seed is always reluctant to be dislodged.

Seed is borne in a number of different ways, and knowledge of these will make life simpler for the seed collector. The easiest seed to collect is that which is not carried in any kind of capsule, as with members of the daisy family (Compositae) and the grasses, where it is designed to be blown away by the wind. This seed can simply be gathered

up and stuffed into a paper bag. Capsule- or pod-borne seed is best gathered by picking whole stems with seed heads intact and holding them upright until you can invert them into a bag. Store the stalks upside down, and the seed will fall out as it dries. Sometimes, as with lilies and irises, this does not happen and it will need to be detached from the capsule with a fingernail.

Few perennials produce berries or fleshy fruit, although many shrubs do. Separating seed from fruit is messy and often very finicky. The flesh often contains germination inhibitors, so remove as much as possible, difficult though this may be. Try soaking the whole berry and then if the seeds do not come out with finger nails, experiment with various kitchen gadgets such as sieves, pestle and mortar or blenders. Remember, though, that many berries are toxic.

The worst seeds to collect are those of plants such as geraniums where the seed head is like a spring that is designed to shoot the seeds as far as possible as soon as they are ripe. The key is to spot the dark seeds that are almost ripe and then to pick the whole head firmly and pop it into a bag, being careful that none shoots into your eyes.

Storing seed

Once harvested, seed should be dried in a well-ventilated place at no more than room temperature, in paper bags or envelopes. Damp seed will rapidly deteriorate in storage. Cleaning involves separating the seed from the chaff (bits of capsule, 'packing material', the fluff of wind-borne seeds,

Capsules (left) *are the most common way that perennials hold seed, and are best collected by picking whole stems and seedheads. Exposed seed and berries* (right) *can be pulled off by hand. Geraniums* (top right) *have seed on springs which has to be picked before it dries out.*

insects etc). For our purposes it does not have to be as clean as you would expect to get from a seed packet; just remove the bulk of extraneous material. The easiest method is to pour the seed on to a piece of paper and then use a card held at ninety degrees to the paper to drag away the usually larger or lighter chaff. Beware sudden draughts or sneezing while doing this.

After cleaning, seed may be stored in paper bags or envelopes in a cool dry place until needed. In the case of those species that need cool treatment (see pages 122-3), you can sow almost immediately. Where you need seed to be stored for any period of time, it is worth considering putting it in the fridge (not the freezer), ideally in an airtight container with some silica gel to act as a gentle dehydrating agent. Storage like this may ensure good germination many years hence.

Growing plants from seed

PEOPLE ACCUSTOMED TO SOWING the seed of plants well established in cultivation are in for a rude shock when it comes to sowing the seed of wildflowers and perennials. Some, to be sure, comes up straight away, but many kinds germinate only sporadically; some may not appear for a year, and the odd recalcitrant batch will not be seen until the year after next. Seed that has been stored (however well) often takes much longer to germinate than fresh seed, which is another reason why sowing your own is such a boon – you can sow it as soon as it is collected. However, this is only part of the story; wild plants have a number of ingenious mechanisms to delay germination until such a time as the seedlings can make a safe start in life. Such mechanisms are not in the gardener's favour, so understanding them and manipulating them is an important part of growing wildflowers from seed.

Many herbaceous perennials that come from climates with a predictably warm spring and summer do germinate easily, as do nearly all annuals and many fast-growing species, such as members of the daisy family (Compositae). Those from cooler climates have a much greater tendency to need a spell of warmth, followed by cold, followed by warmth, before they will germinate. In other words they need a warm autumn spell before a cold winter one before they chemically 'know' it is safe to emerge. Some species further complicate this by not coming up until two cold spells have past.

It is often possible to predict how seeds will behave by knowing their botanical family, or the environment they come from. If you do not know, the best thing to do is to sow in autumn, when the seed is fresh, and protect during winter anything that does germinate immediately. If you cannot be sure of being able to look after them over winter, sow half in autumn and save the rest until spring. Those that you know need a cold spell should be sown in autumn; the average winter will chill the seed sufficiently to enable it to come up in the spring. If this does not happen, do not despair, but save the seed tray for at least another two years (making sure you use an indelible label – pencil is best). It is a constant source of amazement and joy how much can come up two or three years later.

However, it may not be possible for you to get seed until the end of the winter, making natural chilling difficult and recourse to the fridge necessary. To save space (and cater for the desire of the rest of the family to store food), seed should be mixed with a small quantity of sand and just moistened (not soaked) and then popped into a plastic bag. Do not forget a label! The seeds should be kept in a warm (15-20°C/58-66°F) place for four weeks. Check them weekly, just in case a few seedlings do what they are not meant to and come up early. Then keep them at around 3°C/37°F in the fridge for six weeks before sowing them, preferably in a seed tray in a cool shaded place outside.

Germinating seeds

The following is an approximate guide to the seed germination requirements of the more important perennial families:

(1) Germination rapid at around 20°C/66°F, but also good at a bit less:
Campanulaceae (bellflower family)
Caryophyllaceae (pink family)
Compositae/Asteraceae (daisy family)
Cruciferae/Brassicaceae (cabbage and wallflower family)
Euphorbiaceae (spurge family)
Geraniaceae (geranium family)
Gramineae/Poaceae (grass family)
Labiatae/Lamiaceae (mint family)
Malvaceae (mallow family)
Papaveraceae (poppy family)
Rosaceae (rose family – herbaceous species)
Rubiaceae (bedstraw family)
Scrophulariaceae (foxglove family)
Thalictrums
Verbenaceae (verbena family)

(2) Germination best at around 5-10°C/42-50°F, sometimes erratic, and can be inhibited at higher temperatures:
Dipsacaceae (scabious family)
Primulaceae (primrose family) – usually fast and good, but some very slow

(3) Germination after minimum of 4 weeks' warmth, 6 weeks' cold:
Ranunculaceae (buttercup family) – cold spell should be at a few degrees below zero (i.e. the freezer if spring-sown). EXCEPT aquilegias, clematis, thalictrums (see group 1) and hellebores, cimicifuga (see group 4).
Gentianaceae (gentian family)
Iridaceae (iris family)
Liliaceae (lily family) and most bulbous plants – but note individual lily species have widely different requirements, so consult a specialist book.
Rosaceae (rose family – shrubby species)
Saxifragaceae (saxifrage family)
Umbelliferae/Apiaceae (parsley family) – can be very erratic

(4) Two warm/cold spells needed (i.e. two years):
Cimicifuga
Hellebores – unless very fresh; if so, they should be sown immediately, when germination is rapid without chilling
Peonies
Tricyrtis

(5) Hard seeds of Leguminosae/Fabaceae (pea family) need to be mechanically abraded and/or soaked before sowing. The best way is to put them in a jar and pour just-boiled water over them, leaving them to soak for a day. Those that swell should be sown, to germinate within days. Separate out any that do not swell (often a very fiddly job), abrade them either with sandpaper or by quick bursts in a kitchen grinder, and then soak.

Seed sowing

Seedlings are very vulnerable to fungus diseases, which can rapidly destroy whole trays. Use sterilized compost, preferably mixed with grit or perlite (a white rock derivative with great aerating properties, rather like geological popcorn) to minimize the danger of waterlogging, which will encourage fungal infection.

Seed should always be covered, unless it is very fine (like campanula or lobelia seed), when it should be scattered on to sieved compost and gently watered with a watering can to ensure good contact between the seed and the compost.

Some seed needs darkness to germinate, some light. The best compromise in my experience is a layer of fine gravel or chippings; it holds the seed down on to the damp compost, but does not entirely eliminate light. It also reduces moss growth.

Unless you know something to be quick germinating, it is best to enclose the seed trays in plastic bags, to keep out foraging rodents and drifting weed seeds. Put them in a well shaded spot outside, checking weekly for germination. Even in winter you will be surprised how much comes up. Once they have germinated, the seedlings should be moved to a place where they can be safely protected from slugs and from extreme weather conditions, which includes direct sunlight.

Plantings, like this, that require large numbers of individual plants can be expensive. However, the poppies (Papaver orientale), *the lupins, the small mauve* Geranium pyrenaicum *and the purple aquilegias can be rapidly grown from seed. The alliums can also be grown this way, although they are slow, while the pink spikes of* Persicaria bistorta *can be easily propagated by division (see pages 124-5).*

123

Cuttings and division

WHILE GROWING FROM SEED always involves genetic mixing, so that every new plant is slightly different, vegetative methods of propagation like cuttings and division produce new plants identical to the parents. This may be useful in preserving the characteristics of particularly desirable individuals – named cultivars, for instance. Cuttings and divisions are, of course, essential as a means of propagating plants which for any reason do not set seed in the garden. These methods also produce plants that are a suitable size for planting out much more quickly than seed. Propagation is a fascinating business, and much can be gained from a specialist book on the subject, or better still, by learning from other gardeners or nursery owners.

Cuttings

Cuttings are the main method used to propagate woody and semi-woody plants, although herbaceous perennials may be raised this way, too. For our purposes taking cuttings is particularly useful for building up numbers of the shrubby plants that are the backbone of the Mediterranean-climate dry land garden – lavenders, cistuses, artemisias and so on, as well as the heathers, rhododendrons and blueberry relatives of the heathland garden.

Shrubby plants in general are best propagated from 'semi-ripe' growth – stems that are young and full of growth hormones, but not so soft that they wilt easily. Only experience, trial and error and good note-taking will teach you what is ideal material. Early to midsummer is often the best time, after the first flush of growth, but before ripening and hardening of stems has begun. Take cuttings in several batches, over several weeks or months, and record the success rate for future reference. You may find that every species has its own ideal time.

Herbaceous plants are best propagated in spring, just as growth starts. Species that are suitable are those that produce true leafy stems from the base of the plant, such as campanulas, salvias and most members of the daisy family. Unsuitable are those which produce only tufts of leaves and flower stems from the top of the rootstock, such as aquilegias, eryngiums, hellebores and geraniums (most of the latter can be reproduced by division, though). The new season's shoots are packed with growth hormones and will usually root and grow

Many perennials can easily be propagated from cuttings. For heel cuttings (top), carefully pull off young shoots from the main stem with your fingers, so that a strip of stem comes away with it. For semi-ripe cuttings (middle), cut a side shoot from a shrubby plant with a sharp tool. Remove the lower leaves from the cuttings (far left) and dip the base in a small container of rooting powder. Insert the cuttings into a prepared pot of cutting compost (left).

amazingly quickly, much more so than stem cuttings of woody plants. It is often possible and easier to peel cuttings off the hard base of the plant rather than to cut with a knife. These cuttings come with a portion or 'heel' of bark attached, giving the name of 'heel cutting' to this kind of propagation. Some herbaceous plants such as salvias, verbenas and lobelias can be propagated by stem cuttings taken later in the season, too, except when stems have become hollow and the growth has lost its vigour.

The knife or secateurs for taking cuttings should always be very sharp and clean. Methylated spirits or a flame can be used to sterilize cutting tools between batches. Cuttings compost must be made up from sterile material and must be free-draining and well aerated. Perlite should be mixed in 50:50 if at all possible; its aeration effect can make a dramatic difference to success rates. If not available, use sharp grit instead. Once a tray or pot of cuttings is complete, watered and labelled, it should be placed in a cool, shaded place and kept moist. Lacking roots, cuttings are terribly vulnerable to drying out. Putting them into a plastic bag will keep them humid, but also encourages decay, often on a grand and messy scale. Bags should only be used if it seems absolutely necessary to stop wilting; be sure to check the contents every few days and remove all dead or mouldy material.

Division is the most important method of propagating perennials that produce multiple shoots from the base. Dig up the clump, and if it is small or loose enough, separate it into smaller parts by hand (right). *Large or older clumps may need a combination of brute force and tools such as spades or forks. To break up a large, matted, fibrous-rooted clump, insert two forks back-to-back and gradually force them apart* (far right).

Division

This is a ridiculously easy method of propagating plants, but only suitable for herbaceous plants that produce multiple shoots from the base, forming clumps or mats of growth. (Types which have only a single root like a carrot – such as many eryngiums and aquilegias – cannot be divided.) Creeping plants like bugles (*Ajuga* species), which send out shoots that then root at some distance to the parent, rather in the manner of strawberries, can clearly be cut up into lots of new pieces. Those with rhizomes – thickened horizontal roots from which new shoots arise vertically – are also fairly obvious candidates; with bearded irises, Solomon's seal (*Polygonatum* species) or *Geranium endressii*, you can carefully cut the rhizome in such a way as to ensure that each piece has a shoot or bud and some roots. Tight, clump-forming plants do not make it so evident, yet even they can produce large numbers of divisions from one three- or four-year-old plant.

Muscle-power and a certain amount of daring are needed to tear apart a tough woody perennial. The clump should be dug up and, if you are unsure of the shape of the roots, washed clean of soil to help you see

what you are doing. It needs to be torn apart so that it breaks along the lines of least resistance and then further pulled apart to produce as many pieces as possible that have both a piece of root and a stem or bud. Smaller divisions or those with very little root will need more looking after at the beginning, whereas larger ones can be planted out in their final positions. If the plant seems singularly recalcitrant, try prising it apart with two forks or use a sharp knife to cut off suitable pieces of root.

Division can usually be done at any time during the dormant season, from autumn through to the beginning of growth in the spring. A few species are sensitive to winter rotting, though, and good timing is necessary for others, irises and grasses in particular. If at all unsure, leave until spring before taking action.

Growing on young plants

SEEDLINGS, ROOTED CUTTINGS, small divisions and other young plants all need careful looking after in the first few months of life, to nurture them to a size where they can fend for themselves in the garden. Such close care and attention can be given either in a nursery bed or in pots. Both have advantages and disadvantages.

A nursery bed is an area of well-cultivated and weed-free soil, best slightly shaded, where young plants are grown on until they are big enough to plant out. Its advantage over pots is that plants are less vulnerable to drying out and the unlimited root room allows plants, herbaceous perennials particularly, to grow rapidly into good-sized plants which often establish much more quickly in the garden than container-grown ones. Its disadvantage is that pests and diseases can be more of a problem than when plants are grown in pots.

While young cuttings and divisions too small to be planted out directly can be put straight into a nursery bed, all but the largest seedlings will need to be potted up first into small pots before they are large enough for open soil. Seedlings (and rooted

cuttings, too) should be potted on well before their roots become entangled. Much damage can be done trying to separate the roots of seedlings left too long in their trays. Ideally, seedlings should go into individual pots, so that when they are transplanted again they will suffer minimal root disturbance. If you move them into a nursery bed as soon as possible, the larger sizes of commercial nursery plug trays are ideal for this intermediate stage, allowing a large number of seedlings to be grown on in a small space.

Growing plants on in containers allows you to control their environment much more than when they are in a nursery bed – to move them around, for instance. It is arguably perhaps more suitable for woody plants than growing on in a nursery bed, as they take less time to recover from transplanting than do herbaceous species and so the vastly reduced root disturbance involved in planting out from pots allows quicker establishment. Pots and compost cost money, however, and making a nursery bed can be much more cost-effective. Containers, too, are totally dependent upon being watered, which is time-demanding.

Another disadvantage of containers is that they expose plant roots to extremes of temperature. In summer even well-watered plants can be killed if the roots are overheated. This can be avoided if the plants are kept out of direct sun, and also if they are kept close together so that the sides are not exposed to the sun. Keeping pots packed together is even more important in winter, when plants in pots can easily be frozen all the way through on a night when only the top few centimetres of soil in the garden are frozen. Square pots which fit tightly together are ideal, but round ones will need to have straw packed between them or to be covered in insulation material if you expect very low temperatures.

If you do decide to grow your young plants

on in containers, litre or half-litre ones (approximately 1½pt or ¼pt pots) are usually sufficient for one season's growth, although more substantial and vigorous plants may be better in much larger pots.

Plug trays

An alternative to conventional pots, particularly useful if you are growing very large numbers of plants, are the nursery plug trays already mentioned. Seedlings can be pricked out into the larger-sized cells and grown on, to be planted out direct, or into a nursery bed for growing on. Young plants rapidly fill plug trays, but because each plant has its own root space and is not tangled up with its neighbours, as in a seed tray, it is possible to keep herbaceous perennials in plug trays for months, long after they look as if they should have been repotted. In natural environments seedlings often germinate but are unable to grow into full-size plants because of the proximity of the neighbours, staying in a kind of stasis until an opportunity presents itself, a neighbouring plant dying or being eaten for instance, which gives it the chance to mature. Keeping plants ticking over in small containers (almost a kind of bonsai) is thus perfectly natural and does not affect their health or ability to develop normally when planted out. However, you should ensure that they are kept on a hard surface to prevent them from rooting through the holes in the bottom, and periodically water them with plant food.

LEFT *Thousands of plants can be raised cheaply and kept for months in plug trays.*

RIGHT *The plants in this exuberant scene are the result of home propagation followed by planting out the next year, the sage from cuttings, the day lily from division, and the valerian and the thistle from seed.*

Weed and pest control

IN THE NEW PERENNIAL garden there are two approaches to weed control, 'extensive' and 'intensive'. In the wilder grass-based communities like meadows and prairies, the surface of the ground is very largely covered by grasses and perennials and the ground is never disturbed, except by the occasional mole or bird. The vegetation acts as a kind of seal on the surface and the weed seed bank stays buried and out of harm's way. The annual disturbance-tolerating weeds are not a problem after the first two years, because mowing prevents them from seeding and what seed there is cannot come up. Mowing is thus the process that limits weed growth, and it is vital that it is carried out before weed species set seed, even if this means also cutting back on flowering perennials.

Mowing limits the spread and further reproduction of annual weeds and those perennial weeds like docks that produce large amounts of seed. Many other perennial weeds have their growth limited by mowing, which gives plants that can tolerate mowing a competitive advantage. In areas which are not allowed to grow too tall, the wildflower lawn for example, or spring-flowering meadows which are kept mown short for much of the year, mowing alone can almost eliminate the worst weeds. However, in meadow and other taller-grass habitats this is not so effective in the short term, and the gardener may have to resort to more intensive weeding practices. In the longer term, where mowing clippings are being taken away to reduce soil fertility, weeds will be at a disadvantage compared with the species we want to encourage and will gradually die out. Weeds, being vigorous competitive growers, flourish on fertile soils, particularly those with a high nitrogen and phosphorus content which are often the result of past agricultural or horticultural practices such as manuring and fertilizing.

Plantings that do not have a grass matrix – the more conventional features of the new perennial garden such as open borders – need traditional intensive weeding. Weeds are much more obtrusive in this kind of environment, and need to be removed or dealt with on an individual basis. An established planting should have few weed problems once the growth of the plants forms a continuous cover to the soil, as in a meadow. Before this stage is reached, in the early years, and in spring before the herbaceous plants have emerged, weed growth may well be a problem. This is why mulches, which cover the surface and prevent light reaching weed seed on the soil, are so useful. However, unless a synthetic total cover mulch such as black plastic has been used (see pages 126-9), perennial weeds will not be affected.

On soils where it is practicable, and where there is sufficient space between plants, hoeing will eliminate seedlings and eventually eradicate those perennial weeds such as bindweed and couch grass that keep on regenerating from buried roots. The word 'eventually' should be stressed, though! More effective is hand-digging of weeds; hand-pulling is even more rapid where this is possible, which is often the case with newly germinated annuals.

Considerably quicker to carry out than digging, and avoiding the soil disturbance that results in more weed seed germination, is the very careful use of the weedkillers discussed on page 115. Systemic weedkillers such as glyphosate, which reach the whole root system from an application on one part of the victim's surface, can be used for spot-weeding. In particularly difficult cases where danger of spillage on to the wrong plant is possible, a solution of glyphosate can be mixed with wallpaper paste and painted individually on to the leaves of offending plants. Weeds that are not seriously affected by this chemical can be treated by others, although you need to be completely certain that what you use will not harm neighbouring plants. Ammonium sulphamate seems safe in this and in other respects and will even kill brambles.

Pests and diseases are simply not the problem in the new perennial garden that they are in the conventional one. In the first place the occasional slug-chewed leaf or rust-infected flower head is not as conspicuous in a naturalistic garden as in the more ordered layout, just as a few weeds do not stand out nearly as much. The intermingling of varieties and the diversity of a good nature-inspired garden helps, too; if one species is having a bad year, there should be enough near neighbours looking good to make up for it. In addition, pest and diseases are quite often simply not so acute. Natural species often have fewer disease problems than artificially bred hybrids, and with a better and more thorough mix of plants there is less chance of disease and pests spreading. The monocultures so characteristic of certain conventional gardens (rose borders, bedding schemes made up from just five varieties and so on) are ideally suited to the spread of troubles that can affect the whole population of a specific plant.

Plant selection is an important part of the avoidance of problems. By choosing plants that occur naturally in the conditions prevailing in your garden, you are selecting species that are unlikely to be put under stress, and stress is the open door for plant disease. Monardas, for example, are renowned by gardeners as martyrs to mildew, a result of their being grown in

conditions slightly too dry for them. Yet if grown in the constantly moist ground that they (and many of the related hybrids derived from *M. didyma*) need, then mildew is unlikely to appear.

There is no denying that you may still have problems. Large-scale pests include rabbits and deer. Both can be excluded by fencing, but this may be too expensive or undesirable. They are both highly selective eaters, deer especially so, and trial and error can yield a selection of plants they do not care for. Various bitter-tasting potions are available to spray on to vulnerable plants to discourage them, which certainly seems to

work in the case of rabbits.

Slugs and snails are perhaps the most destructive of all, so much so that in perfectly natural conditions they can cause local extinctions of wild plant species in wet spring weather. New plantings and susceptible plants (generally those with soft, hairless or fleshy foliage) must be protected. Ploys include encircling vulnerable plants with gravel or ash, using traditional saucers of beer as slug traps, and the judicious and minimal scattering of slug pellets. Once plants are established, however, the ravages of these pests are usually greatly reduced, and in normal circumstances local wildlife –

Damp ground needs a mix of robust perennials to form a successful low-maintenance plant community – plants such as Iris sibirica, *comfrey* (Symphytum), *red campion* (Silene dioica) *and cranesbills* (Geranium). *Well-blended naturalistic planting like this means that if any one species is badly affected by pests one year, the overall effect is unchanged.*

toads, birds, hedgehogs and so on – will deal with the worst of them. You should always aim for a natural balance if possible.

Maintenance and mowing

NORMAL GARDEN ROUTINES – pruning, weeding, staking, cutting back and so on – amount to so-called intensive maintenance, applied to plants on an individual basis. Features of the new perennial garden such as the open border, where there is no grass matrix, will need to have some of this kind of treatment, although the amount of intervention needed will usually be far lower than in traditional borders. Plantings with a grass matrix such as meadows and prairies are maintained on an extensive basis, in which all the plants are treated in the same way and all together. Whereas in a border we can thin out or divide plants that have got too big, it is impracticable in a grassy habitat; in fact it often does more harm than good, as every time that the ground is disturbed it opens the door to opportunist weed seeds to come and germinate.

A grass-based planting is a community of plants which is in a constant state of flux, with a natural dynamism about it that a border lacks. The weather conditions one year will benefit some species at the expense of others; next year different conditions may favour different species. Our mowing schedule will be one of the factors that affects this constant and subtle interplay.

Suppose we have a meadow that we want to keep fairly short, tidy and full of spring flowers like cowslips, pasque flowers (*Pulsatilla* species) and small bulbs. The grass is allowed to grow until after these plants have set seed, which will be roughly a few weeks after midsummer's day. The grass is then mown to around 4 cm/1½in (somewhat higher than a conventional lawn) and kept that low for the rest of the year. Leaving it uncut would only benefit larger

species and vigorous grasses which might displace the spring flora.

In later-flowering meadows, certain species may need to be held in check – grasses, for instance, or the sometimes too-vigorous ox-eye daisy – so time your mowing to take place after their main flowering season, to stop them setting seed. In this case the meadow would also be mown soon after midsummer, but then allowed to grow again, to give later-flowering knapweeds (*Centaurea* species) and scabious (*Scabiosa* and *Knautia* species) an opportunity to bloom. This encourages certain plants like yarrows (*Achillea* species) to flower again.

Mowers used for cutting meadows should be of the sort where it is possible to raise the cutting height higher than that used for a traditional lawn. Cutting too low may damage some wildflowers. For meadows where low-fertility plants are encouraged, a grass box is useful for removing cuttings. Otherwise much labour-intensive raking will be necessary.

Prairies and wetland plantings will produce growth that is too tall and tough for a mower to cope with. A traditional scythe may be used, or a strimmer, or (on a large scale) a mini-tractor with a flail.

More conventional plantings without a grass matrix, such as the open border, will need the kind of maintenance that gardeners are used to; weeding, and occasional thinning out of larger herbaceous plants. Cutting back on a large scale can be done all at once, though, with a strimmer if necessary. Wetland plantings without a grass matrix will need this kind of care, too. The lush growing conditions may encourage a lot of weed growth at first, but once established the rank growth of moisture-loving perennials usually needs only an annual end-of-year cutting back.

Shrubby heathland plantings usually need little attention, as the plants intermesh well

enough to discourage weeds and their slow growth has little need for constant cutting back. If pruning is needed, it should be carried out after flowering. Dry-land plantings, where growth rates are low and most plants fairly static, need this kind of maintenance too, although not usually very much of it. Spaces between plants tend to be greater than in moister environments, which can lead to some weeding.

The existence of prairies in nature is closely tied to their vegetation being frequently burnt off, and it has been found that burning is the best way of maintaining artificial prairie plantings. It eliminates invading weedy plants and reduces the growth of the more vigorous species like some of the goldenrods. Needless to say, it is a maintenance tool that needs to be very carefully handled, and a prairie manual or landscape specialist (and perhaps the fire department) should be consulted before you strike the first match.

Any kind of gardening produces waste material, and if you are seriously trying to reduce soil fertility by removing clippings, then you may find quite a lot on your hands. If you have a vegetable garden or conventional borders with a need for high fertility, then clippings and prunings may be composted. An alternative is to shred them, a particularly useful method for tough stalks and woody stems, and then use the end product as mulching material on borders or around the bases of new plants. If used fresh, the shreddings will deplete the soil of nutrients as they decay; if you compost them, they will add to the soil's fertility.

Prairie coneflower (Ratibida pinnata) *dominates a prairie planting in late summer. This kind of area need be cut only once a year, preferably in late winter, using a strimmer able to cut tough stems.*

Plant Tables

A few of these plants are banned
in Australia; see page 154

KEY

foliage, habit	Sp = Spring	A = Autumn	N = Normal
E = Evergreen	Lsp = Late spring	W = Winter	M = Moist
	Esu = Early summer	Lw = Late winter	D = Dry
	Msu = Midsummer		Sh = Shade
season	Su = Summer	*situation*	Ac = Acid
Esp = Early spring	Lsu = Late summer	W = Wet	Aq = Aquatic

Plants for shade

botanical name	height	foliage, habit	flower	season	situation	zone	remarks
CLUMP-FORMING, SLOWLY SPREADING							
Arum italicum	30cm/12in	paler veins, semi-E	pale green	Sp	N	6	*A. maculatum* similar
Epimedium × warleyense	30cm/12in	glossy, semi-E	small, orange	Sp	M N	5	other species similar
Hosta sieboldiana	60cm/24in	elegant greyish	lilac	Su	M N	3	many similar species/varieties
Iris foetidissima	60cm/24in	dark, linear	orange berries	A	M N	5	good in sun or deep shade
Lathyrus vernus	30cm/12in	dense clumps	pink, blue	Sp	N	5	various colour forms
Pachysandra terminalis	25cm/10in	neat shrubby growth	white	Sp	N	4	best on acid soil
Primula vulgaris	10cm/4in	small rosette	pale yellow	Sp	M N	5	various colour forms
Pulmonaria saccharata	30cm/12in	silver splashed, E	pink, blue	Sp	M N	4	many other species/varieties
Smilacina racemosa	70cm/28in	striking, pleated	cream	Sp	M N	4	other species less dramatic
Tellima grandiflora	30cm/12in	hairy, pale green, E	green	Sp	M N D	4	purple-leaved form especially good
Tiarella cordifolia	15cm/6in	neat, lobed, E	white	Sp	M N	3	best in acid humus
OPEN HABIT, SLOWLY SPREADING							
Actaea alba	80cm/32in	divided	white fruit	A	M N	4	other species similar
Aruncus dioicus	150cm/60in	pale, divided	cream	Su	M N	3	other smaller species/varieties
Cimicifuga racemosa	80cm/32in	divided	white	Su, A	M	3	dislikes competition
Lunaria rediviva	100cm/40in	triangular	lilac	Sp	M N	3	short-lived, but self-seeds
Meconopsis cambrica	40cm/16in	pale green	yellow	Su	N	6	short-lived, but self-seeds
Polygonatum × hybridum	60cm/24in	elegant, arching	white	Su	N	4	other similar species
GROUND COVER, VIGOROUSLY SPREADING							
Asarum europaeum	10cm/4in	glossy, heart-shaped	insignificant		M N	5	other similar species
Astilbe chinensis var. *pumila*	25cm/10in	dark, divided	pink	Su	M N	4	
Euphorbia amygdaloides var. *robbiae*	40cm/16in	glossy, dark green	yellow	Sp, Lw	M D	8	very tolerant, can be invasive
Hedera helix	20cm/8in	dark green, E	insignificant		N D	6	many variegated forms
Lamium maculatum	20cm/8in	silver splashed, E	pink, white	Sp	N D	3	various varieties
Lamium galeobdolon	30cm/12in	silver splashed, E	small, yellow	Sp	M N	4	can be invasive ['Florentinum']
Petasites albus	30cm/12in	large, heart-shaped	white	Esp	M N	5	particularly rampant spreader
Symphytum grandiflorum	25cm/10in	coarse	cream	Sp	N D	5	other species mostly blue
Vinca minor	15cm/6in	glossy, E	blue	Sp	N D	4	*V. major* similar, larger
Waldsteinia ternata	10cm/4in	shiny, semi-E	yellow	Sp	N D	3	*W. geoides* similar

botanical name	height	foliage, habit	flower	season	situation		zone	remarks
GRASSES, SEDGES AND RUSHES								
Carex pendula	70cm/28in	arching clumps, E	catkin-like	Su	M N		5	self-seeds strongly
Luzula sylvatica	30cm/12in	shiny, E	cream	Su	M N		3	thrives on acid; other similar spp.
Melica uniflora	30cm/12in	fresh green	nodding	Su	N		5	lawn-like ground cover
Milium effusum	100cm/40in	light yellowish	pale green	Su	N		5	yellow forms
BULBS AND OTHER SUMMER-DORMANT PLANTS								
Anemone nemorosa	10cm/4in	small, divided	white	Sp	N		4	needs humus
Convallaria majalis	20cm/8in	rich green	white	Sp	N		4	good spreader
Corydalis solida	15cm/6in	small, divided	pink	Sp	N		6	can self-seed
Cyclamen hederifolium	10cm/4in	intricate markings	pink, white	Su, A	N D		5	can self-seed
Cyclamen repandum	10cm/4in	dark green	deep pink	Sp	N D		7	can self-seed
Eranthis hyemalis	5cm/2in	divided	yellow	Sp	N		4	can self-seed
Erythronium dens-canis	15cm/6in	marbled	pink, cream	Sp	N		3	humus rich soil
Galanthus nivalis	10cm/4in	narrow, greyish	white	Sp	W N		4	forms sizeable clumps
Galium odoratum	15cm/6in	small pale green	white	Sp	N D		5	good spreader
Mertensia pulmonarioides	50cm/20in	greyish-green	pale blue	Sp	M N		4	protect from slugs
Sanguinaria canadensis	20cm/8in	greyish, lobed	white	Sp	M N		3	prefers acid humus
Trillium grandiflorum	30cm/12in	lobed	white	Sp	M		4	many other species, slow to increase
FERNS								
Adiantum pedatum	30cm/12in	graceful			M		3	many other species
Asplenium scolopendrium	30cm/12in	undivided, leathery, E			M D		4	remarkably tolerant
Athyrium filix-femina	60cm/24in	delicate fresh green			M		4	
Dryopteris erythrosora	50cm/20in	new growth pink			M N		6	many other species
Dryopteris filix-mas	100cm/40in	sturdy semi-E			N D		4	most robust fern
Matteuccia struthiopteris	100cm/40in	'vase'-shaped habit			M N		2	excellent plant for damp
Onoclea sensibilis	45cm/18in	fresh green			W M		4	spreads rapidly in damp
Polystichum acrostichoides	50cm/20in	dark green, E			M N		3	useful ground cover
Polystichum setiferum	50cm/20in	intricately divided			N D		5	many varieties, tolerant
Thelypteris noveboracensis	40cm/16in	graceful, light green			N		3	powerful spreader in warm areas

Plants for light shade
Most will also thrive in full sun in places where there is no risk of summer drought.

botanical name	height	foliage, habit	flower	season	situation		zone	remarks
TALLER								
Aconitum lycoctonum	80cm/32in	lobed, large	cream	Msu	M N		3	many other *aconitum* species
Anemone sylvestris	40cm/16in	dark green	white	Lsp	N		4	can spread strongly
Anthericum liliago	50cm/20in	grass-like	white	Esu	N D		6	*A. l.* 'Major', similar but stronger
Aquilegia vulgaris	70cm/28in	greyish, divided	blue, pink	Esu	N		5	many similar species, self-seeds
Aster divaricatus	70cm/28in	dark stems	white	Lsu	N D		4	*A. macrophyllus* similar
Astrantia major	80cm/32in	dark	cream	Su	M N		4	also *A. maxima*

botanical name	height	foliage, habit	flower	season	situation	zone	remarks
Campanula latifolia	80cm/32in	loose clumps	mauve-blue	Msu	N D	4	*C. trachelium* similar but smaller
Campanula persicifolia	80cm/32in	rosettes, E	blue, white	Msu	N D	4	especially good on sand
Dictamnus albus	80cm/32in	aromatic divided	pink, white	Esu	N D	3	especially good on sand
Digitalis lutea	70cm/28in	rosettes, E	pale yellow	Msu	N D	4	many similar yellow/brown species
Digitalis purpurea	150cm/60in	rosettes, E	white to purple	Su	N D	4	self-seeds; also in sun
Doronicum orientale	50cm/20in	fresh green	yellow daisy	Esu	N	5	other species similar
Eupatorium rugosum	100cm/40in	dark green	white	Lsu, A	N	4	*E. coelestinum* blue (for warm areas)
Euphorbia amygdaloides	50cm/20in	reddish tinge, E	green	Esp, Lw	N D	6	spreads well
Gentiana asclepiadea	50cm/20in	fresh green	blue	Lsu	M	6	acid soil best
Geranium sylvaticum	60cm/24in	lobed	pink, mauve	Esu	M N	4	many colour forms
Lilium martagon	120cm/48in	whorled leaves	pink, purple	Esu	M N	4	can self-seed
Myrrhis odorata	90cm/36in	ferny	white	Esu	M N	4	best 'cow parsley'
Senecio nemorensis	120cm/48in	reddish stems	yellow daisy	Lsu	N	4	difficult to find, but very useful
Silene diqica	60cm/24in	fresh green	deep pink	Esu	M N	5	short-lived, but self-seeds
Silene virginica	60cm/24in	rosettes	crimson	Esu	N	4	short-lived, but self-seeds
Stachys officinalis	50cm/20in	wavy edged leaves	dark pink	Su	N	4	other stachys species similar
Succisa pratensis	60cm/24in	dark green	mauve	Lsu	M N	5	prefers moist, peaty soils
Telekia speciosa	150cm/60in	large, impressive	yellow daisy	Msu	M N	5	*Buphthalmum salicifolium* similar

CLUMP-FORMING

botanical name	height	foliage, habit	flower	season	situation	zone	remarks
Alchemilla mollis	40cm/16in	elegant, lobed	green-yellow	Esu	M N D	4	can self-seed invasively
Bergenia cordifolia	30cm/12in	large, red in winter	pink	Sp	M N D	3	very tolerant
Brunnera macrophylla	40cm/16in	large, heart-shaped	blue	Lsp	M N	4	several variegated forms
Chrysogonum virginianum	30cm/12in	variable growth	yellow daisy	Sp, Esu	N	6	several forms available
Coreopsis auriculata	30cm/12in	lobed	yellow daisy	Lsp	N	4	forms vary in size
Dicentra eximia	30cm/12in	greyish green, ferny	pink, white	Su	M N	4	several similar species/varieties
Geranium endressii	60cm/24in	fresh green	pink	Su	M N	4	very reliable
Geranium himalayense	40cm/16in	dark green	blue	Su	M N D	4	good spreader
Geranium macrorrhizum	40cm/16in	lobed	pink, white	Esu	N D	4	strong weed suppressor

Pulmonaria saccharata

Lamium maculatum

Erythronium dens-canis

botanical name	height	foliage, habit	flower	season	situation		zone	remarks
Geranium phaeum	50cm/20in	lobed	maroon, purple	Lsp	N		4	many colour forms
Geranium sanguineum	40cm/16in	lobed	magenta, pink	Esu	N D		4	many colour forms
Helleborus foetidus	80cm/32in	impressive, lobed, E	greenish	Lw	N D		6	can self-seed
Helleborus niger	50cm/20in	lobed, E	white	Lw	N D		4	many other species/varieties
Viola riviniana	7cm/3in	small, dark	violet	Esp	N		5	many other species/varieties

GROUND COVER, SPREADING

botanical name	height	foliage, habit	flower	season	situation		zone	remarks
Ajuga reptans	10cm/4in	shiny dark green	clear blue	Sp	M N		3	various cultivars
Buglossoides purpurocaerulea	20cm/8in	grey-green	clear blue	Lsp	N D		6	very vigorously spreading
Clematis × jouiniana	30cm/12in	sprawling	pale blue	Su	N		5	spreads to 2-3m/6-10ft
Glechoma hederacea	15cm/6in	soft, hairy	mauve-blue	Esu	M N		4	tolerates mowing; can be invasive
Lamium galeobdolon	30cm/12in	fresh green	yellow	Esu	M N		4	
Omphalodes verna	15cm/6in	light green	clear blue	Sp	M N		5	spreads slowly
Phlox stolonifera	30cm/12in	trailing stems	pink, blue	Esu	N	Ac	3	*P. divaricata* similar

BULBS

botanical name	height	foliage, habit	flower	season	situation		zone	remarks
Hyacinthoides non-scripta	20cm/8in	broadly grassy	blue	Lsp	N	Ac	4	*H. hispanica* similar
Leucojum aestivum	60cm/24in	grassy	white, green tips	Lsp	M N		4	several similar species
Narcissus pseudonarcissus	25cm/10in	broadly grassy	yellow	Lsp	N		4	innumerable hybrids
Scilla siberica	15cm/6in	broadly grassy	blue	Sp	N		3	other species similar

Plants for moist shade

The following need light shade unless Sh indicated, when they will tolerate full shade. All can be grown in sun in moist soils.

botanical name	height	foliage, habit	flower	season	situation		zone	remarks
TALL, UPRIGHT								
Aconitum lycoctonum	80cm/32in	lobed, large	cream	Msu	M N		4	many other aconitum species
Anemone × hybrida	100cm/40in	dark, divided	pink, white	Lsu, A	M N	Sh	5	many varieties
Artemisia lactiflora	150cm/60in	narrow upright growth	cream	Su	M N		4	

Campanula latifolia alba

Myrrhis odorata

Geranium endressii

Plants for moist shade

botanical name	height	foliage, habit	flower	season	situation	zone	remarks
Aruncus dioicus	150cm/60in	pale, divided	cream	Su	M N	3	other smaller species/varieties
Campanula lactiflora	150cm/60in	robust clumps	pale blue	Su	M N	4	several colour forms
Cimicifuga racemosa	80cm/32in	divided	white	Su, A	M	3	dislikes competition
Filipendula camtschatica	150cm/60in	divided	cream	Su	M N	3	
Ligularia dentata	100cm/40in	rounded	yellow daisy	Su	M N	4	several similar species
Lilium martagon	120cm/48in	whorled leaves	pink, purple	Esu	M N	4	can self-seed

MEDIUM, UPRIGHT

botanical name	height	foliage, habit	flower	season	situation	zone	remarks
Actaea alba	80cm/32in	divided	white fruit	A	M N	4	other species similar
Aster divaricatus	70cm/28in	dark stems	white	Lsu	N D	4	*A. macrophyllus* similar
Astilbe chinensis var. *pumila*	25cm/10in	dark, divided	pink	Su	M N	4	
Astrantia major	80cm/32in	dark	cream	Su	M N	4	also *A. maxima*
Gentiana asclepiadea	50cm/20in	fresh green	blue	Lsu	M	6	acid soil best
Geranium sylvaticum	60cm/24in	lobed	pink, mauve	Esu	M N	4	any colour forms
Lunaria rediviva	100cm/40in	triangular	lilac	Sp	M N	3	short-lived, but self-seeds
Matteuccia struthiopteris	100cm/40in	'vase'-shaped			M N	2	excellent plant for damp
Myrrhis odorata	90cm/36in	ferny	white	Esu	M N	4	best 'cow parsley'
Silene dioica	60cm/24in	fresh green	deep pink	Esu	M N	5	short-lived, but self-seeds
Succisa pratensis	60cm/24in	dark green	mauve	Lsu	M N	5	
Telekia speciosa	150cm/60in	large, impressive	yellow daisy	Su	M N	5	*Buphthalmum salicifolium* similar

CLUMP-FORMING

botanical name	height	foliage, habit	flower	season	situation	zone	remarks
Alchemilla mollis	40cm/16in	elegant, lobed	green-yellow	Esu	M N D	4	can self-seed invasively
Astilbe hybrids	70cm/28in	divided	red, pink, white	Su	M N Sh	4	large number of varieties
Astilbe chinensis var. *pumila*	25cm/10in	dark, divided	pink	Su	M N	4	
Brunnera macrophylla	40cm/16in	heart-shaped	blue	Sp	M N	4	
Carex pendula and many other carex species	70cm/28in	arching clumps, E	catkin-like	Su	M N	5	self-seeds strongly
Dicentra eximia	35cm/14in	greyish green, ferny	pink, white	Su	M N	4	
Geranium endressii	45cm/18in	light green	pink	Su	M N	4	
Geranium himalayense	45cm/18in	dark green	blue	Su	M N	4	
Hemerocallis lilioasphodelus	70cm/28in	sword-shaped	clear yellow	Esu	M N	3	innumerable hybrids
Hosta sieboldiana	60cm/24in	elegant greyish	lilac	Su	M N	3	
Onoclea sensibilis	45cm/18in	fresh green		Sp, Su, A	W M	4	spreads rapidly in damp
Primula elatior	20cm/8in	small rosette	pale yellow	Sp	M N	5	
Primula florindae	70cm/28in	rosette	yellow scented	Su	W M N	6	
Primula japonica	60cm/24in	rosette	pink, white	Esu	M N	6	many similar species

Plants for meadows

botanical name	height	foliage, habit	flower	season	situation	zone	remarks
LOW-GROWING							
Campanula rotundifolia	15cm/6in	insignificant	blue	Su	N D	3	dislikes competition
Centaurium erythraea	15cm/6in	insignificant	bright pink, tiny	Su	N D	3	dislikes competition
Lotus corniculatus	15cm/6in	dark green, divided	yellow, pea-like	Esu	N D	5	
Muscari neglectum	15cm/6in	grassy	dark blue	Lsp	N D	4	bulbs
Primula veris	15cm/6in	low rosette, E	yellow	Sp	N D	5	one of the best spring plants
Thymus serpyllum	5cm/2in	tiny, aromatic, E	dark pink	Su	D	5	many related species
Trifolium pratense	15cm/6in	three-lobed, E	reddish pink	Esu	M N	3	avoid agricultural varieties
MEDIUM							
Anthemis tinctoria	50cm/20in	finely divided	yellow daisies	Su	D	4	can be short-lived
Anthyllis vulneraria	30cm/12in	compact	yellow, pea-like	Su	D	5	can be short-lived
Aster amellus	50cm/20in	upright	violet	Lsu	N D	5	various garden varieties
Dianthus carthusianorum	50cm/20in	insignificant	deep pink, red	Su	D	3	showy
Eryngium campestre	50cm/20in	spiny	green-white	Su	D	5	
Euphorbia cyparissias	30cm/12in	finely divided	greeny-yellow	Su	D	3	can be invasive
Filipendula vulgaris	50cm/20in	finely divided	creamy-white heads	Esu	N D	4	best on dry soils
Galium verum	40cm/16in	finely divided	yellow heads	Su	N D	3	sprawling, best on dry soils
Hippocrepis comosa	20cm/8in	divided	yellow, pea-like	Esu	D	6	
Iris graminea	30cm/12in	grassy	pale violet	Esu	D	5	
Jasione laevis	30cm/12in	dark green	dark mauve-blue	Su	N D	5	
Linaria vulgaris	30cm/12in	sprawling	yellow 'snapdragons'	Su	D	4	
Linum perenne	25cm/10in	insignificant	pale clear blue	Esu	D	4	
Narcissus poeticus	50cm/20in	linear	white, yellow centre	Sp	N	5	bulbs
Ononis repens	20cm/8in	compact growth	strong pink	Su	M N D	6	best on drier soils
Origanum vulgare	30cm/12in	neat aromatic foliage	dull pink	Su	D	4	
Phyteuma orbiculare	30cm/12in	insignificant	deep blue spiky heads	Esu	M N D	6	
Pilosella aurantiaca	25cm/10in	tight mats of leaves	dull orange	Esu	M N	4	can be invasive
Prunella vulgaris	20cm/8in	low growing	violet-purple	Su	M N D	6	
Pulsatilla vulgaris	20cm/8in	feathery	violet, large, bell-shaped	Sp	D	3	spectacular, various colours
Sanguisorba minor	40cm/16in	greyish, divided	green and red round heads	Esu	D	5	
Scabiosa columbaria	40cm/16in	rosettes	pale pinky mauve	Su	N D	5	
Sedum telephium	40cm/16in	fleshy greyish	dull pink	Lsu	N D	4	excellent butterfly plant
Stachys officinalis	50cm/20in	wavy edged leaves	dark pinky	Su	M N	4	very attractive *en masse*
Veronica austriaca subsp. *teucrium*	30cm/12in	fresh green	clear blue	Esu	M N D	5	
TALLER							
Achillea millefolium	60cm/24in	dark, feathery, E	white clusters	Su	M N D	3	very adaptable, may be invasive
Aristolochia clematitis	60cm/24in	mid green, elegant	pale yellow 'pipes'	Su	N D	5	

botanical name	height	foliage, habit	flower	season	situation	zone	remarks
Aster linosyris	60cm/24in	finely divided	yellow	Lsu	D	3	
Campanula glomerata	60cm/24in	rough textured	purple-blue	Esu	N D	3	spreads
Centaurea nigra	60cm/24in	basal rosettes	pink-purple	Su	N D	5	very adaptable
Centaurea scabiosa	70cm/28in	basal rosettes	carmine-pink	Su	D	4	very showy
Cichorium intybus	80cm/32in	upright	clear blue	Su	N D	4	can be short-lived
Daucus carota	80cm/32in	dark, finely divided	off-white heads	Su	N D	3	short-lived, but often seeds
Geranium pratense	70cm/28in	lobed	mauve-blue	Su	M N D	4	best on poorer soils
Hypericum perforatum	60cm/24in	erect growing stems	yellow	Su	N	3	
Knautia arvensis	60cm/24in	basal rosettes	pale pinky-mauve heads	Su	N D	6	
Lathyrus pratensis	70cm/28in	divided	yellow pea-like	Esu	M N	4	several other species
Leucanthemum vulgare	60cm/24in	dark green	white & yellow daisies	Esu	M N D	3	short-lived, seeds on dry soils
Malva moschata	60cm/24in	pale green, divided	pale pink, large	Su	N D	4	can be short-lived
Malva sylvestris	100cm/40in	sprawling	large showy pink	Su	N D	5	short-lived, can self-seed
Onobrychis viciifolia	60cm/24in	divided	strong dusky pink	Esu	M N D	6	
Polemonium caeruleum	60cm/24in	divided	clear blue	Esu	M N	4	can seed itself widely
Ranunculus acris	70cm/28in	dark green	bright yellow	Lsp, Su	M N D	4	very easy, adaptable plant
Salvia pratensis	60cm/24in	rough-textured, dark	deep blue-violet, showy	Su	N D	3	classic limestone plant
Silene latifolia	60cm/24in	upright	creamy-white	Esu	M N	3	
Verbascum phoeniceum	60cm/24in	dark, rosette	violet	Esu	D	5	many colour forms

CLIMBERS/TRAILERS

botanical name	height	foliage, habit	flower	season	situation	zone	remarks
Galium mollugo	100cm/40in	sprawling	foaming white	Su	M N D	3	
Vicia cracca	80cm/32in	divided	blue-purple	Su	N	3	climber/scrambler

Plants for rough grass

botanical name	height	foliage, habit	flower	season	situation	zone	remarks
Acanthus mollis	90cm/36in	elegant foliage, dense clumps	maroon and white	Su	N D	7	grows best in warm areas
Achillea millefolium	60cm/24in	strongly creeping	white	Su	M N D	3	
Alchemilla mollis	40cm/16in	elegant, lobed	green-yellow	Esu	M N D	4	
Althaea officinalis	140cm/56in	tall, bushy	pale pink	Lsu	M N	5	
Aquilegia vulgaris	70cm/28in	self-seeds	violet, blue	Esu	N	5	
Aruncus dioicus	150cm/60in	tall, robust clumps	cream	Su	M N	3	
Asclepias syriaca	200cm/80in	spreading rhizomes	pink	Su	N D	3	spreads strongly on light soil
Aster novae-angliae	150cm/60in	creeping, self-seeds	lavender	Lsu, A	M N	4	
Buglossoides purpurocaerulea	20cm/8in	sprawling stems	blue	Esu	N	6	
Campanula lactiflora	150cm/60in	robust clumps	pale blue	Su	M N	4	
Campanula rapunculoides	100cm/40in	invasive rhizomes	violet-blue	Su	N D	3	notoriously invasive
Centaurea macrocephala	90cm/36in	solid, robust clumps	yellow	Su	N	3	

botanical name	height	foliage, habit	flower	season	situation	zone	remarks
Centaurea montana	50cm/20in	slowly spreading	violet-blue	Esu	N	3	various forms available
Centaurea nervosa	100cm/40in	robust clumps	pink-mauve	Su	N	4	many similar wild·species
Centaurea nigra	60cm/24in	small clumps, self-seeds	mauve-pink	Su	N D	5	
Cephalaria gigantea	250cm/100in	tall, robust clumps	pale yellow	Su	M N	3	
Clematis × jouiniana	30cm/12in	sprawling	pale blue	Su	N	5	several other similar species
Coreopsis tripteris	200cm/80in	tall, robust clumps	yellow daisies	Su, A	M N	4	
Coronilla varia	30cm/12in	sprawling	pink	Esu	N	3	good on banks and bare soil
Crambe cordifolia	180cm/72in	large, dark green clump	clouds of white	Esu	N D	6	several similar species
Crocosmia							
× *crocosmiiflora*	70cm/28in	spreading	orange	Lsu	N D	6	other forms, but less vigorous
Doronicum pardalianches	90cm/36in	spreading strongly	yellow	Sp	N	4	tolerates light shade
Echinops exaltatus	170cm/68in	tall, robust clumps	bluish	Su	M N	3	several similar species
Eupatorium purpureum	250cm/100in	tall, robust clumps	pink	Lsu	M N	3	
Euphorbia characias	150cm/60in	bushy, grey foliage	yellow-green	Sp, Lw	N D	7	also tolerates shade
Euphorbia griffithii	70cm/28in	slowly spreading clumps	reddish	Esu	N D	4	tolerates some shade
Filipendula rubra	200cm/80in	large clumps, elegant foliage	purple-pink	Su	M	3	tolerates some shade
Foeniculum vulgare	150cm/60in	robust clump, fine foliage	yellow-green	Su	N D	4	also good purple leaved form
Galega officinalis	140cm/56in	upright bushy	pale mauve	Su	N	4	tolerates some shade
Galega orientalis	120cm/48in	strongly spreading root	pure blue	Esu	N	5	
Geranium × oxonianum							
'Claridge Druce'	80cm/32in	weed-smothering clumps	deep pink	Esu	M N	4	several similar varieties
Geranium phaeum	50cm/20in	lobed, clumps	maroon, pink	Lsp	M N	4	
Geranium pratense	70cm/28in	strong upright growth	mauve-blue	Su	M N	4	
Geranium psilostemon	90cm/36in	bushy upright growth	magenta	Esu	M N	4	
Inula magnifica	200cm/80in	tall, spreads slowly	yellow daisies	Su	M N	4	several similar species
Iris pseudacorus	150cm/60in	robust clumps	yellow	Esu	M N	5	
Leucanthemella serotina	150cm/60in	tall, robust clumps	white daisies	Lsu	M N	4	
Ligularia dentata	100cm/40in	tall, spreads slowly	yellow daisies	Su	M N	4	
Lupinus Russell Hybrids	100cm/40in	self-seeds	wide range	Esu	N	3	short-lived but spectacular
Macleaya cordata	250cm/100in	tall, spreads, elegant foliage	flesh-coloured	Esu	M N	4	spreads quickly on moist ground
Papaver orientale	80cm/32in	coarse, hairy	large, red	Esu	N D	4	summer dormant
Phytolacca polyandra	120cm/48in	tall, self-seeds	pink, and fruit	Su, A	M N	6	toxic: several other species
Persicaria amplexicaulis	120cm/48in	bushy	deep pink	Lsu	M N	5	several varieties
Persicaria bistorta	80cm/32in	dock-like, spreading	pink	Esu	M N	4	
Rheum palmatum							
'Atrosanguineum'	180cm/72in	clump of large elegant foliage	red	Esu	M N	5	several similar species
Rodgersia podophylla	150cm/60in	large, bronze	cream	Su	M	5	
Rudbeckia 'Juligold'	180cm/72in	tall, robust clump	yellow daisies	Lsu	M N	3	*R. laciniata* similar
Salvia glutinosa	100cm/40in	tall, robust clump	pale yellow	Su	N	5	tolerates some shade
Saponaria officinalis	80cm/32in	rapidly spreading	pink	Su	N	4	tolerates some shade
Sinacalia tangutica	150cm/60in	strongly spreading	yellow	Su	M N	6	attractive seed heads

botanical name	height	foliage, habit	flower	season	situation	zone	remarks
Solidago canadensis	100cm/40in	strongly spreading	yellow	Lsu, A	N	3	many less invasive species
Symphytum grandiflorum	25cm/10in	dense spreading clumps	blue	Lsp	M N	5	
Tanacetum vulgare	120cm/48in	tall, spreading	yellow buttons	Su	N	3	
Thalictrum flavum							
subsp. *glaucum*	200cm/80in	tall, robust clumps, grey	yellow	Esu	W M N	6	tolerates some shade
Verbascum 'Vernale'	180cm/72in	robust clumps	yellow	Su, A	M N	5	self-seeds
GRASSES AND SEDGES							
Arundo donax	300cm/120in	tall, slowly spreading clumps, E			M	7	best in warmer climates
Carex pendula	70cm/28in	arching clumps	brown 'catkins'	Su	M N	5	self-seeds
Elymus arenarius	100cm/40in	grey foliage, spreading	insignificant		N D	4	invasive in light soil
Miscanthus sinensis	180cm/72in	robust clumps	silver flowers	Lsu, A	M N	5	slow to establish, self-seeds
Phalaris arundinacea	90cm/36in	invasive spreader, E			M N	4	variegated form more common
Spartina pectinata	150cm/60in	arching, spreading	insignificant	Su, A	M N	5	also variegated form

Plants for prairies

botanical name	height	foliage, habit	flower	season	situation	zone	remarks
LOW GROWING, TO 50-60 cm/20-24 in							
Allium cernuum	60cm/24in	linear	pink	Lsu	M N D	3	bulbous
Baptisia bracteata	100cm/40in	greyish, elegant	cream	Su	N	5	slow to mature
Dodecatheon meadia	25cm/10in	low rosette	pink	Esu	N	5	tolerant of light shade
Euphorbia corollata	60cm/24in	bushy growth	white	Su	N D	3	long flowering season

Lotus corniculatus

Centaurea montana

Inula magnifica

botanical name	height	foliage, habit	flower	season	situation	zone	remarks
Geum triflorum	25cm/10in	very divided	maroon	Sp, Su, A	M N D	3	attractive woolly seed heads
Liatris cylindracea	60cm/24in	compact growth	pink-violet	Su, A	D	3	best on dry soils
Pulsatilla patens	30cm/12in	finely divided	white-pink	Sp, Esu	N	5	
Zizia aptera	60cm/24in	dark, attractive	yellow	Sp	N	3	foliage particularly good

Grasses

botanical name	height	foliage, habit	flower	season	situation	zone	remarks
Koeleria macrantha	60cm/24in			Su	D	3	

MEDIUM, TO 50-150 cm/20-60 in

botanical name	height	foliage, habit	flower	season	situation	zone	remarks
Asclepias incarnata	90cm/36in	architectural	pink	Su		3	can be invasive
Asclepias tuberosa	80cm/32in	dark, upright	orange	Su	M N D	4	useful for hot, dry soils
Aster ericoides	80cm/32in	masses of tiny leaves	white	La	D	3	useful for late flower
Aster laevis	60cm/24in	upright	blue-purple	Lsu	M N D	4	
Aster ptarmicoides	190cm/76in	compact	white	A	D	3	
Baptisia lactea	150cm/60in	blue-green, waxy	white	Esu	M N	5	can be slow to mature
Chelone glabra	90cm/36in	dark green	pink	Lsu	M	3	dislikes drought
Echinacea pallida	120cm/48in	coarse	purple	Esu	N	4	long-lived
Eryngium yuccifolium	120cm/48in	yucca-like	white	Lsu	M N	4	
Eupatorium perfoliatum	100cm/40in	lush	white	Lsu	M	3	
Iris virginica var. *shrevei*	80cm/32in	sword-like	blue	Lsp	M	5	slow to flower from seed
Liatris aspera	80cm/32in	low growth	pink-violet	Lsu	N D	4	seeds popular with birds
Liatris pycnostachya	110cm/44in	linear	purple	Su	M	4	
Lilium superbum	150cm/60in	upright	orange	Su	M	5	slow to flower from seed

Monarda

Filipendula purpurea

Salvia sclarea

Plants for prairies

botanical name	height	foliage, habit	flower	season	situation	zone	remarks
Lobelia siphilitica	100cm/40in	upright	blue	Su	M	5	long-lived
Monarda didyma	90cm/36in	aromatic, wandering	scarlet	Lsu	M	4	
Monarda fistulosa	120cm/48in	aromatic, wandering	lavender	Lsu	M N D	3	
Monarda punctata	100cm/40in	aromatic, branched	pale yellow	Su	D	6	short-lived, but seeds
Oenothera biennis	130cm/50in	sprawling	yellow	Su	M N D	4	short-lived, but seeds
Parthenium integrifolium	100cm/40in	upright	white	Su	M N	5	
Penstemon grandiflorus	120cm/48in	branching	pale purple	Lsp, Su	D	3	endangered in the wild
Petalostemon purpureum	110cm/44in	divided	pink-violet	Su, A	N D	4	
Ratibida pinnata	180cm/72in	upright	yellow	Msu	N D	3	one of the most striking
Rudbeckia hirta	80cm/32in	lance-shaped	yellow	Su	N D	3	short-lived, but seeds
Rudbeckia subtomentosa	120cm/48in	upright	yellow	Lsu	N	5	
Solidago rigida	120cm/48in	upright	yellow	Lsu, A	M N D	3	not invasive like some
Verbena stricta	120cm/48in	coarse	blue-mauve	Su	M N D	3	drought tolerant
Veronicastrum virginicum	150cm/60in	stiffly upright	white	Lsu	M N	4	statuesque plant

Grasses

botanical name	height	foliage, habit	flower	season	situation	zone	remarks
Bouteloua curtipendula	80cm/32in	narrow		Su, A	N D	3	only competes on dry soils
Schizachyrium scoparium	110cm/44in	blue, green hues		Su, A	N D	3	one of two 'basic' grasses
Sporobolus heterolepsis	100cm/40in	compact		A	N D	3	good for soil stabilization

TALLER, TO 200 cm/6 ft

botanical name	height	foliage, habit	flower	season	situation	zone	remarks
Asclepias syriaca	200cm/80in	distinctive	pink	Su	N D	3	monarch butterfly food source
Aster novae-angliae	180cm/72in	upright	purple	A	M N	4	can be invasive
Coreopsis palmata	180cm/72in	stiff, upright	yellow	Su	N D	3	good for poor sandy soils
Coreopsis tripteris	200cm/80in	bushy	yellow	Su, A	M N	4	long flowering season
Desmodium canadense	190cm/76in	clover-like leaves	pink	Su	M N	3	
Eupatorium purpureum	250cm/100in	bulky, shrub-like	pink	Su	M	3	adored by butterflies
Filipendula purpurea	200cm/80in	single upright stems	pink	Su	M	3	
Helianthus angustifolius	180cm/72in	coarse, thin	yellow	Su	M N D	6	many similar species
Heliopsis helianthoides	170cm/68in	upright-growing	yellow	Su	M N	4	very easy and fast
Lespedeza capitata	180cm/72in	clover-like leaves	mauve	Su, A	N D	5	
Silphium laciniatum	300cm/120in	very tall	yellow	Lsu	M N	5	
Vernonia crinita	250cm/100in	dark	pink-violet	Lsu, A	M	5	looks good with yellows

Grasses

botanical name	height	foliage, habit	flower	season	situation	zone	remarks
Andropogon gerardii	300cm/120in	good autumn colour		Su, A	M N D	3	the other essential grass
Calamagrostis canadensis	180cm/72in	tufted		Su	M	3	
Elymus canadensis	180cm/72in	bristled		A	M N D	4	good 'nurse' crop for seeds
Panicum virgatum	200cm/80in	good autumn colour		Su, A	N D	5	good for general garden use
Sorghastrum avenaceum	200cm/80in	majestic		Su, A	N D	3	quickly maturing
Spartina pectinata	150cm/60in	long, arching		Su, A	M N	5	can be invasive on wet ground

Plants for heathland

botanical name	height	foliage, habit	flower	season	situation		zone	remarks
Antennaria dioica	10cm/4in	silvery, carpeting, E	pink, on male plants	Esu			2	
Arctostaphylos uva-ursi	10cm/4in	glossy, spreading, E	white, red fruit	Su	N	Ac	3	
Arnica montana	40cm/16in	rosettes of leaves	yellow daisies	Lsp	M N	Ac	6	rather short-lived
Calluna vulgaris	60cm/24in	shrubby, E	pink, red, white	Su	M N	Ac	4	vast choice of varieties
Campanula rotundifolia	15cm/6in	sparse	blue	Su	N D		3	
Chamaedaphne calyculata	30cm/12in	dwarf shrub, E	small white	Sp	N	Ac	2	
Cornus canadensis	15cm/6in	neat oval leaves, E	white	Lsp	N	Ac	2	best in some shade
Daboecia cantabrica	50cm/20in	heather-like, E	pink bells	Su	N	Ac	5	
Dianthus arenarius	15cm/6in	grass-like, E	white fragrant	Esu	N		3	
Dianthus deltoides	15cm/6in	grass-like, E	pink	Su	N		3	spreads readily
Digitalis purpurea	150cm/60in	rosettes	white to purple	Esu	N D		4	
Erica carnea	40cm/16in	shrubby, E	red, pink, white	Esp	W N		5	lime-tolerant, many varieties
Erica ciliaris	30cm/12in	low-growing, E	bright pink	Su	N	Ac	7	
Erica cinerea	30cm/12in	low-growing, E	dark pink	Su	N	Ac	6	
Erica erigena	100cm/40in	shrubby, E	dark pink	Sp	N	Ac	8	somewhat tender
Gaultheria cuneata	30cm/12in	textured leaves, E	white berries	Su	N'	Ac	6	
Gaultheria mucronata	80cm/32in	prickly shrubs, E	white, pink berries	Lsu, A	M N	Ac	6	male & female needed for fruit
Gaultheria procumbens	15cm/6in	glossy, mat-forming, E	white, red fruit	Su	N	Ac	4	
Genista tinctoria	60cm/24in	dwarf shrub, E	yellow, pea-like	Sp, Su	N		5	
Gentiana sino-ornata	5cm/2in	mat of light green, E	blue trumpets	Lsu, A	N	Ac	6	rampant in cool conditions
Kalmia angustifolia f. *rubra*	70cm/28in	rounded shrub, E	pink, in bunches	Esu	M N	Ac	2	
Ledum groenlandicum	70cm/28in	dense shrub, E	white	Lsp	M N	Ac	2	
Phyllodoce caerulea	30cm/12in	heath-like shrub, E	small pink bells	Lsp	N	Ac	3	
Pilosella officinarum	10cm/4in	hairy leaves	yellow daisies	Sp	N		5	
Rhododendron racemosum	60cm/24in	dense shrub, E	pink, in bunches	Lsp	N	Ac	5	many other species
Salix reticulata	5cm/2in	mat of textured foliage	tiny catkins	Sp	N		1	likes cool conditions
Thymus serpyllum	5cm/2in	tiny, aromatic	dark pink	Su	N D		3	
Vaccinium vitis-idaea	20cm/8in	small glossy leaves, E	white, red fruit	Su	N	Ac	2	many similar species

GRASSES

botanical name	height	foliage, habit	flower	season	situation		zone	remarks
Carex buchananii	70cm/28in	tufts of brown, E		Su	N		6	
Carex muskingumensis	80cm/32in	bright green, E	brown	Su	M		7	very distinctive
Deschampsia flexuosa	50cm/20in	tufted, fine leaves	airy panicles	Su	N	Ac	4	
Festuca ovina	30cm/12in	grey-green tufts, E	blue-green	Su	M N		4	
Koeleria glauca	30cm/12in	blue-green	tight, fawn heads	Esu	D		4	
Molinia caerulea	70cm/28in	dark greyish tufts	purplish heads	Su	M N		5	

botanical name	height	foliage, habit	flower	season	situation	zone	remarks
FOR BOGGY CONDITIONS (acid, wet and very low fertility)							
Andromeda polifolia	20cm/8in	delicate twiggy shrub, E	white, pink	Sp	W M	Ac 3	
Carex glaucescens	110cm/44in	bluish clumps, E	pendent spikes		W M	Ac	
Dactylorhiza majalis	20cm/8in	spotted leaves	deep purple pink	Esu	W M	Ac 5	
Helonias bullata	80cm/32in	strap-shaped	pink spike	Lsp	W	Ac 6	
Myrica gale	150cm/60in	shrubby, aromatic	red-brown	Sp	W M	Ac 1	
Parnassia palustris	15cm/6in	glossy rosette	white	Su	W M	Ac 5	
Rhexia virginica	50cm/20in	textured	bright pink	Su	W M	Ac 3	
Rhinanthus serotinus	50cm/20in	narrow	pale yellow	Esu	M N	6	
Sarracenia flava	50cm/20in	funnel shaped	yellow	Sp	W	Ac 7	insectivorous
Vaccinium macrocarpon	5cm/2in	carpets of wiry stems, E	red berries	Su	M	Ac 2	

Short-lived perennials, biennials and annuals

botanical name	height	foliage, habit	flower	season	situation	zone	remarks
SHORT-LIVED PERENNIALS (often biennial)							
Alcea rosea	200cm/80in	coarse, fresh green	pink, red, yellow, brown	Esu	N	3	many colour forms
Anchusa azurea	120cm/48in	coarse, dark	strong blue	Esu	N D	4	
Digitalis purpurea	150cm/60in	rosettes	white to purple	Su	N D	4	
Erysimum hieraciifolium	25cm/10in	bushy	bright orange	Lsp	N	7	
Gaillardia × grandiflora	60cm/24in	sprawling	large yellow daisies	Su	D	3	needs poor soil
Hesperis matronalis	90cm/36in	coarse, dark	pale lilac, scented	Esu	M N	4	tolerates some shade
Lunaria rediviva	75cm/30in	branching growth	purple or white	Sp		6	
Meconopsis cambrica	40cm/16in	clumps, deeply lobed	yellow	Su	N D	6	
Myosotis sylvatica	40cm/16in	bushy	light blue	Sp, Esu	M N	5	
Rudbeckia triloba	90cm/36in	bushy	yellow, dark centres	Lsu	N	3	free-flowering
Tanacetum parthenium	40cm/16in	light green, divided	white and yellow	Su	N	4	
Verbena bonariensis	110cm/44in	rather sparse	violet heads	Lsu	N	9	excellent butterfly plant
BIENNIALS							
Angelica gigas	110cm/44in	dark green, lobed	large maroon-purple heads	Su	M N	6	
Campanula patula	50cm/20in	rather sparse	mauve-blue bells	Esu	M N	6	
Cynoglossum amabile	40cm/16in	greyish	clear blue	Esu	M N	7	tolerates some shade
Dipsacus fullonum	150cm/60in	rough-textured	thistle-like	Su	N D	3	elegant in winter
Echium vulgare	70cm/28in	rough-textured	deep blue spikes	Su	D	3	biennial, but usually seeds
Eryngium giganteum	110cm/44in	basal rosette	white, thistle-like	Su	N	6	
Euphorbia lathyrus	120cm/48in	very erect	pale yellow	Su	N	6	tolerates some shade
Geranium robertianum	60cm/24in	red-tinged, sticky	bright pink	Esu	M N	3	shade-tolerant, seeds madly
Glaucium flavum	60cm/24in	greyish	yellow, poppy-like	Su	N D	5	
Isatis tinctoria	120cm/48in	greyish	large heads of yellow	Esu	N	7	
Linaria genistifolia	60cm/24in	grey	yellow 'snapdragons'	Su	N D	4	

botanical name	height	foliage, habit	flower	season	situation	zone	remarks
Lychnis coronaria	80cm/32in	grey, woolly	magenta	Esu	N	4	white and pink forms, too
Lychnis viscaria	35cm/14in	sparse	vivid yellow	Esu	D	3	
Onopordum acanthium	200cm/80in	grey, spiny	pink red	Su	N	5	vast and magnificent
Salvia sclarea	90cm/36in	rough-looking	leafy pink bracts	Su	N D	5	blue and white forms, too
S. s. var. turkestanica	120cm/48in	large, coarse, furry	large pinky-white spike	Su	N D	5	
Silybum marianum	100cm/40in	white-streaked,	spiny purple thistles	Su	N	7	
Smyrnium perfoliatum	100cm/40in	lush green	greeny-yellow heads	Lsp	N	8	good buffer colour
Verbascum bombyciferum	200cm/80in	covered in white fur	yellow spires	Su	N D	6	magnificent, seeds freely

ANNUALS

botanical name	height	foliage, habit	flower	season	situation	zone	remarks
Agrostemma githago	100cm/40in	erect	mauve	Su	N		self-seeds prodigiously
Borago officinalis	40cm/16in	very hairy	clear blue	Esu			
Centaurea cyanea	80cm/32in	sparse foliage	dark blue heads	Su	N D		
Chrysanthemum segetum	80cm/32in	lobed	yellow daisies	Su	N		
Clarkia amoena	80cm/32in	erect	bright pink	Su	N D		
Collinsia heterophylla	60cm/24in	velvety	lavender blue and white	Su	M N		tolerates some shade
Coreopsis tinctoria	90cm/36in	feathery	yellow, red centres	Su	N D		
Eschscholzia californica	30cm/12in	feathery	orange, poppy-like	Su	N D		
Layia platyglossa	20cm/8in	compact	yellow, edged white	Su	N D		
Limnanthes douglasii	15cm/6in	light green	white and yellow	Su	N D		
Linum grandiflorum							
'Rubrum'	40cm/16in	greyish	dark red	Su	N		
Lupinus texensis	50cm/20in	multi-lobed	vivid blue	Su	N D		
Mentzelia lindleyi	40cm/16in	toothed	yellow	Su	N D		
Nemophila insignis	30cm/12in	bushy	blue	Su	N D		
Nigella damascena	40cm/16in	very finely divided	blue, pink, white	Su	N		
Papaver rhoeas	60cm/24in	divided, hairy	scarlet	Su	N D		
Papaver somniferum	100cm/40in	greyish, fleshy	red, pink, white, purple	Su	N D		many colour forms
Phacelia tanacetifolia	90cm/36in	dark leaves, erect	mauve blue	Esu	N D		
Phlox drummondii	40cm/16in	compact	dark red	Su	N		
Rhinanthus minor	30cm/12in	narrow	pale yellow	Esu	N D		semi-parasite on grass
Rhinanthus serotinus	50cm/20in	narrow	pale yellow	Esu	M N		semi-parasite on grass
Scabiosa atropurpurea	80cm/32in	erect bushy	very dark red	Su	N		
Silene armeria	50cm/20in	erect	magenta	Su	N D		

Plants for moist ground

botanical name	height	foliage, habit	flower	season	situation	zone	remarks
SMALLER							
Ajuga reptans	10cm/4in	shiny, dark green, E	clear blue	Sp	M N	3	
Alchemilla mollis	40cm/16in	very dense clumps	lime green	Esu	M N D	4	
Astilbe chinensis var. *pumila*	25cm/10in	ferny, purplish	feathery, pink	Su	M N	4	
Astilbe hybrids	45cm/18in	divided and toothed	whites, pinks or reds	Su	M N	4	
Cardamine pratensis	25cm/10in	insignificant	palest lilac	Sp	M	4	
Centaurea jacea	50cm/20in	rough-textured	dark pinky mauve	Su	M N	5	
Geum rivale	30cm/12in	tight rosette	small red-brown	Su	W M	3	
Leucojum aestivum	60cm/24in	grassy	white with green tips	Lsp	M N	4	
Lychnis flos-cuculi	30cm/12in	basal rosette	pink, fringed petals	Esu	M	3	can seed prolifically
Potentilla anserina	20cm/8in	silvery, divided	yellow	Su	M	4	useful low-growing plant
Primula elatior	25cm/10in	small rosette	pale yellow heads	Sp	M N	5	
Primula florindae	70cm/28in	rosette	rounded, yellow	Su	W M N	6	
Serratula tinctoria	60cm/24in	divided	small violet heads	Lsu	M N	5	
Silene dioica	60cm/24in	fresh green	rose-red	Esu	M N	5	
Succisa pratensis	75cm/30in	dark green	mauve	Su, Lsu	M N	5	
Trollius europaeus	50cm/20in	dark green, lobed	golden, globular	Esu	W M	4	various colour forms

Trollius europaeus

Astrantia major

Mentha longifolia

botanical name	height	foliage, habit	flower	season	situation	zone	remarks
LARGER							
Artemisia lactiflora	180cm/72in	narrow upright growth	cream	Su	M N	4	
Aruncus dioicus	180cm/72in	tall, robust clumps	cream	Su	M N D	3	
Asclepias incarnata	110cm/44in	distinctive	pale pink, scented	Esu	M N	3	
Astrantia major	80cm/32in	dark	cream	Su	M N	4	
Boltonia asteroides	210cm/84in	greyish	white daisies	Lsu	M N	4	
Camassia cusickii	90cm/36in	linear	blue spikes	Lsp	M N	3	
Carex pendula	120cm/48in	dense clumps	pendulous flowers	Esu	M N	5	
Chelone obliqua	80cm/32in	dark green	pink spikes	Su	M N	4	also for light shade
Cirsium oleraceum	80cm/32in	large leafy clump	creamy bracts	Su	M N	5	useful buffer for brighter colours
Cirsium rivulare	70cm/28in	large leafy clump	bright pink-purple	Su	W M N	4	
Eupatorium cannabinum	100cm/40in	erect coarse stems	pale pink	Lsu	M N	3	shade tolerant
Filipendula camtschatica	200cm/80in	palmate	pale pink	Su	M	3	
Filipendula ulmaria	100cm/40in	erect	cream, fragrant	Su	W M N	3	easy and attractive
Geranium psilostemon	90cm/36in	bushy, upright	magenta, dark centres	Esu	M N	4	
Helenium autumnale	110cm/44in	erect clumps	yellow daisies	Su	W M	4	many hybrids available
Helianthus angustifolius	200cm/80in	narrow	yellow daisies	Su	M N D	6	
Hemerocallis							
lilioasphodelus	75cm/30in	lax, sword-shaped	clear yellow, fragrant	Lsp	M N	3	

Physostegia virginiana

Thalictrum aquilegiifolium

Lobelia cardinalis

147

botanical name	height	foliage, habit	flower	season	situation	zone	remarks
Iris sibirica	80cm/32in	linear	blue-violet	Esu	M N	4	many named varieties
Ligularia dentata	120cm/48in	tall, spreads slowly	yellow daisy	Su	M N	4	
Lilium martagon	150cm/60in	whorls	pink, purple	Esu	M N	4	
Lobelia siphilitica	100cm/40in	erect	blue spikes	Su	M	5	
Lysimachia vulgaris	120cm/48in	erect	deep yellow	Esu	W M	5	
Lythrum salicaria	120cm/48in	erect	deep magenta-pink spikes	Su	W M N	3	banned in N. America
Mentha longifolia	70cm/28in	grey	pale pink	Su	W M N	6	
Miscanthus sinensis	240cm/96in	bold grassy clumps	silvery spikes	Lsu, A	M N	5	many smaller forms
Persicaria amplexicaulis	120cm/48in	large bushy	deep pink, long spikes	Lsu	M N	5	
Persicaria bistorta	80cm/32in	dock-like	pink heads	Esu	M N	4	vigorous
Petasites albus	30cm/12in	large, heart-shaped	white	Sp	M N	5	
Phlox paniculata	180cm/72in	bushy shape	pale pink	Su	M N	4	parent of garden hybrids
Physostegia virginica	70cm/28in	erect	bright pink	Su	M N	4	can be invasive
Rudbeckia laciniata	200cm/80in	coarsely toothed	yellow	Su	M N	3	tolerates some shade
Rudbeckia maxima	190cm/76in	bluish basal leaves	yellow, black centres	Lsu	M N	6	very dramatic
Sanguisorba officinalis	100cm/40in	divided	small dark red heads	Su	W M	4	effective en masse
Telekia speciosa	120cm/48in	large, impressive	yellow daisies	Su	M N	5	
Thalictrum aquilegiifolium	100cm/40in	elegantly divided	fluffy pink heads	Esu	M N	5	
Thalictrum flavum subsp. *glaucum*	200cm/80in	as above but greyish	soft yellow heads	Esu	W M N	6	
Valeriana officinalis	90cm/36in	sparse foliage	palest pink heads	Su	W M	5	
Veronica longifolia	80cm/32in	neat clumps	pale blue spikes	Su	W M N	4	

Aquatics and plants for the waterside

botanical name	height	foliage, habit	flower	season	situation	zone	remarks
FOR WATERLOGGED SOIL (including very shallow water)							
Acorus gramineus	20cm/8in	grassy	insignificant	Sp	W	5	
Aruncus dioicus	180cm/72in	tall, robust clumps	cream	Su	M N D	3	
Astilbe hybrids	45cm/18in	divided and toothed	whites, pinks or reds	Su	M N	4	
Caltha palustris	40cm/16in	glossy green	large yellow 'buttercups'	Sp	W M	4	
Carex pendula	120cm/48in	dense clumps	pendulous	Esu	M N	5	
Cyperus longus	130cm/52in	glossy, arching	red-brown	Su	W	4	
Filipendula camtschatica	200cm/80in	palmate	pale pink	Su	M	3	
Hibiscus moscheutos	80cm/32in	erect	large pink flowers	Lsu	W M	5	
Leucojum aestivum	60cm/24in	grassy	white with green tips	Lsp	M N	4	
Ligularia dentata	120cm/48in	tall, spreads slowly	orange	Su	M	4	
Lobelia cardinalis	80cm/32in	upright growth	scarlet	Lsu	W M N	3	dislikes mild wet winters
Matteuccia struthiopteris	100cm/40in	shuttlecock of fronds			M N	2	
Mimulus guttatus	30cm/12in	fresh green rosettes	yellow, spotted	Su	W M N	6	can seed itself intolerably

botanical name	height	foliage, habit	flower	season	situation	zone	remarks
Myosotis scorpioides	30cm/12in	sprawling	clear blue, long flowering	Su	W	4	
Onoclea sensibilis	45cm/18in	fresh green		Sp, Su, A	W M	4	
Osmunda regalis	200cm/80in	majestic fresh green	brown spore cases	Sp, Su, A	W M	3	shade-tolerant, best on acid
Petasites albus	30cm/12in	large, heart-shaped	white	Sp	M N	5	
Primula florindae	70cm/28in	rosettes	yellow scented	Su	W M N	5	
Primula japonica	60cm/24in	clump-forming	candelabra, various colours	Esu	M N	5	
Rodgersia podophylla	150cm/60in	large, bronzey	cream	Su	M	5	
Saururus cernuus	60cm/24in	heart-shaped	white 'tails'	Su	W	5	shade-tolerant, invasive

also plants on pages 146-7 with W coding

MARGINALS (rooted in soil in shallow water with most of growth above water)

botanical name	height	foliage, habit	flower	season	situation		zone	remarks
Acorus calamus	100cm/40in	sword-like	club shaped	Esu	W		4	can be invasive
Alisma plantago-aquatica	100cm/40in	spoon-shaped	large white panicles	Su	W		5	
Butomus umbellatus	140cm/56in	rush-like	pink on tall stems	Su	W		5	dislikes alkaline soil
Iris laevigata	80cm/32in	upright, strap-like	purple, blue, white	Esu	W M	Aq	4	vast number of varieties
Iris pseudacorus	120cm/48in	upright, strap-like	yellow	Esu	W M N		5	
Iris versicolor	100cm/40in	upright, strap-like	violet	Esu	W M N		4	
Lysichiton americanus	80cm/32in	huge, fresh green	yellow, arum-lily-like	Sp	W		7	
Lysimachia thyrsiflora	80cm/32in	erect growth	yellow	Esu	W M		4	
Mentha aquatica	60cm/24in	erect, aromatic	pale pink, fluffy heads	Su	W M		6	
Pontederia cordata	70cm/28in	glossy, dark	blue spikes	Lsu	W		4	
Ranunculus lingua	100cm/40in	grey-green	large yellow buttercups	Esu	W		4	can be invasive
Sagittaria latifolia	150cm/60in	arrow-shaped	white	Su, A	W		4	
Sparganium erectum	200cm/80in	tall, upright	insignificant	Su	W		6	can be invasive
Typha minima	60cm/24in	upright, strap-like	upright cylindrical	Su	W		5	related species large/rampant
Veronica beccabunga	30cm/12in	succulent, green	blue	Su	W		5	can be rampant
Zizania latifolia	150cm/60in	sword-like	insignificant	Su, A	W		9	good autumn colour

AQUATICS (rooted in deeper water)

botanical name	height	foliage, habit	flower	season	situation		zone	remarks
Hottonia palustris	floating	underwater	palest pink	Su		Aq	5	
Menyanthes trifoliata	30cm/12in	small, emergent	white, fringed	Su	W M	Aq	3	can survive on dry land
Nelumbo lutea	floating	leaves emergent	yellow	Su		Aq	6	
Nuphar pumila	floating	circular, floating	pale yellow	Su		Aq	4	
Nymphaea alba	floating	circular, floating	white	Su		Aq	6	spreads widely
Nymphoides peltata	floating	small floating	yellow	Su		Aq	5	
Orontium aquaticum	60cm/24in	blue-green	yellow 'clubs'	Sp		Aq	8	
Persicaria amphibia	30cm/12in	small, dark markings	small pink spikes	Su, A	W	Aq	5	can be invasive
Potamogeton pulcher	floating	glossy, floating	insignificant	Su		Aq	5	

Plants for dry environments

botanical name	height	foliage, habit	flower	season	situation	zone	remarks
SHRUBBY							
Artemisia absinthium	80cm/32in	silver, aromatic	insignificant	Su	N D	4	
Ballota pseudodictamnus	60cm/24in	silver-grey, woolly, E	small, pale lavender	Su	N D	8	
Bupleurum fruticosum	150cm/60in	dark green, fleshy E	greeny yellow heads	Lsu, A	N D	7	
Ceanothus thyrsiflorus							
var. *repens*	40cm/16in	dark green, glossy, E	blue, prolific	Esu	N D	8	spreading shape
Cistus laurifolius	100cm/40in	green, oval-shaped, E	white, crepe-paper texture	Esu	N D	8	
Cistus salviifolius	70cm/28in	neat, dark green, E	white	Esu	N D	8	
Genista lydia	45cm/18in	dark green, spiny, E	yellow pea-like	Lsp	N D	7	
Halimium ocymoides	60cm/24in	small, grey, E	yellow, dark centred	Esu	N D	8	spreading shape
Hebe armstrongii	40cm/16in	yellowy, cypress-like, E	white, small	Sp	N D	8	many related species
Hebe pinguifolia	25cm/10in	small blue-green, E	white	Esu	N D	7	
Helianthemum hybrids	20cm/8in	small, spreading, E	yellow, red, white, pink	Esu	N D	5	large number of varieties
Hippocrepis emerus	150cm/60in	blue-green, E	yellow, interesting pods	Su	N D	7	
Hyssopus officinalis	60cm/24in	narrow, aromatic, E	violet	Esu	N D	6	
Lavandula angustifolia	60cm/24in	silver, aromatic, E	lavender	Esu	N D	5	prune after flowering
Lotus hirsutus	50cm/20in	grey, woolly texture, E	white, reddish fruit	Su	N D	8	best cut hard back in autumn
Lupinus chamissonis	90cm/36in	silvery, lobed	blue	Su, A	N D	8	
Melianthus major	200cm/80in	large divided, E	red-brown	Su	N D	9	majestic foliage plant

Lavandula angustifolia

Myrtus communis

Phlomis fruticosa

botanical name	height	foliage, habit	flower	season	situation	zone	remarks
Mimulus aurantiacus	120cm/48in	much branched, E	pale orange	Sp, Su	N D	9	
Myrtus communis	200cm/80in	small, dark, E	white, fluffy	Esu	N D	8	
Penstemon campanulatus	60cm/24in	linear, bushy, E	pink, purple	Lsu	N D	8	vast number of hybrids
Phlomis fruticosa	70cm/28in	grey-green, E	yellow in whorls	Esu	N D	7	
Phygelius aequalis	90cm/36in	dark green, untidy, E	orange red	Su	N D	8	
Prunus tenella	100cm/40in	upright shrub	pink-red, white	Esp	N D	3	shrubby cherry relative
Rosmarinus officinalis	70cm/28in	narrow, aromatic, E	blue	Su	N D	8	
Salvia officinalis	40cm/16in	rounded grey leaves, E	mauve	Esu	N D	5	
Santolina chamaecyparissus	50cm/20in	tiny silvery leaves, E	yellow	Esu	N D	7	
Yucca filamentosa	100cm/40in	rosette of stiff swords, E	cream in massive head	Su	N D	5	
Zauschneria californica	30cm/12in	bushy trailer	orange-red	Su	N D	8	

NON-SHRUBBY

botanical name	height	foliage, habit	flower	season	situation	zone	remarks
Agapanthus campanulatus	100cm/40in	strap-shaped, E	clear blue in bunches	Su	N D	8	
Allium christophii	40cm/16in	grey, strap-shaped	large mauve heads	Esu	N D	4	
Alstroemeria ligtu	80cm/32in	erect	pink, orange	Su	N D	6	
Argyranthemum frutescens	100cm/40in	greyish, divided, E	white daisies	Su	N D	9	
Ceratostigma plumbaginoides	40cm/16in	fresh green, compact	clear blue	Lsu, A	N D	5	good autumn colour
Convolvulus sabatius	20cm/8in	greyish, trailing, E	lavender-blue	Su	N D	9	
Cynara cardunculus	150cm/60in	silver, divided	huge blue 'thistles'	Su	N D	7	

Allium christophii and *Stachys byzantina*

Alstroemeria ligtu and alliums

Perovskia

151

botanical name	height	foliage, habit	flower	season	situation	zone	remarks
Delosperma nubigenum	10cm/4in	succulent, sprawling, E	yellow, daisy-like	Su	D	8	dislikes damp
Echium pininana	250cm/100in	grey in rosette, E	towering spike of blue	Su	N D	9	dies after flowering but seeds
Gaura lindheimeri	80cm/32in	very sparse	white, prolific	Lsu	N D	7	short-lived, but often seeds
Gladiolus communis subsp. *byzantinus*	60cm/24in	sword-like	dark magenta	Esu	N D	7	
Hedysarum coronarium	60cm/24in	divided	pink-red, pea-like	Su	N D	4	
Helleborus argutifolius	80cm/32in	greyish, divided, E	green	Sp, W	N D	7	useful foliage plant
Liriope spicata	30cm/12in	grass-like, E	lavender	Su	N D	4	alternative to grass
Nerine bowdenii	60cm/24in	strap-like	pink heads	A	N D	8	flowers appear before leaves
Onosma stellulata	15cm/6in	hairy, greyish, E	yellow	Esu	D	7	
Osteospermum jucundum	30cm/12in	spreading mats, E	pink daisies	Su	N D	8	one of hardier species
Perovskia abrotanoides	100cm/40in	silvery, upright	rich blue violet	Lsu	N D	6	
Romneya coulteri	200cm/80in	silvery	pure white 'poppies'	Su	N D	8	magnificent
Stachys byzantina	40cm/16in	silver, woolly, E	mauve	Su	N D	4	vigorous
Tulipa praestans	25cm/10in	usual tulip leaves	scarlet	Sp	N D	4	bulb
Tulipa tarda	15cm/6in	glossy	yellow and cream	Lsp	N D	4	bulb

Plants for steppes

botanical name	height	foliage, habit	flower	season	situation	zone	remarks
SMALLER							
Acaena microphylla	5cm/2in	divided, brownish, E	red globular heads	Esu	N D	6	vigorous carpeter
Achillea tomentosa	15cm/6in	grey	yellow heads	Esu	D	3	dislikes damp
Allium oreophilum	15cm/6in	strap-like	dark pink	Lsp	N D	3	
Callirhoe involucrata	15cm/6in	sprawling stems	magenta	Su	D	3	
Iris pumila	15cm/6in	linear leaves, E	blue, yellow centres	Lsp	D	4	
Potentilla alba	10cm/4in	lobed, elegant, E	white	Lsp	N D	5	also yellow flowers
Sedum album	5cm/2in	succulent, E	white	Esu	D	3	
Veronica prostrata	10cm/4in	compact mats	blue	Esu	N D	5	
MEDIUM							
Amsonia orientalis	50cm/20in	pointed	steely violet-blue	Su	N D	5	
Anthemis punctata subsp. *cupaniana*	30cm/12in	silver, divided	white and yellow daisies	Esu	N D	6	vigorous sprawler
Artemisia pontica	50cm/20in	grey, feathery	insignificant		N D	5	can be invasive
Euphorbia myrsinites	20cm/8in	trailing, grey, E	green-yellow	Lsp	N D	5	
Euphorbia polychroma	40cm/16in	compact shape	yellow-green	Lsp	N D	4	
Globularia punctata	20cm/8in	bushy, E	blue globular heads	Lsp	N D	5	
Heterotheca villosa	20cm/8in	greyish	yellow daisies	Su	N D	5	
Inula ensifolia	40cm/16in	bushy	yellow daisies	Su	N D	4	

botanical name	height	foliage, habit	flower	season	situation	zone	remarks
Iris germanica	50cm/20in	wide grey linear, E	large, mauve	Esu	N D	4	vast number of garden hybrids
Limonium latifolium	50cm/20in	basal rosette	tiny lilac bunches	Esu	N D	4	
Marrubium cylleneum	20cm/8in	attractive velvety	insignificant		D	7	
Nepeta × faassenii	50cm/20in	greyish, sprawling	mauve-blue	Esu, A	N D	4	flowers again if cut back
Oenothera missouriensis	20cm/8in	glossy, sprawling	large yellow	Su	N D	5	short-lived but self-seeds
Origanum laevigatum	40cm/16in	aromatic, dark	violet	Lsu	N D	5	
Scabiosa columbaria var. *ochroleuca*	50cm/20in	basal rosette	pale yellow	Su	N D	4	
Tanacetum haradjanii	20cm/8in	silver, feathery, E	insignificant		D	6	lovely but dislikes damp
Teucrium × lucidrys	30cm/12in	compact shape	mauve-purple	Su	N D	6	
Thymus vulgaris	20cm/8in	small, compact, E	pink-purple	Su	N D	5	large number of cultivars

TALLER

botanical name	height	foliage, habit	flower	season	situation	zone	remarks
Acanthus spinosus	80cm/32in	lobed, very elegant	green, purple spikes	Lsu	N D	7	
Allium giganteum	120cm/48in	grey linear	purple globular	Esu	N D	6	dramatic and stylish
Asphodeline lutea	70cm/28in	grassy grey rosette	yellow spikes	Esu	N D	6	
Catananche caerulea	60cm/24in	basal rosettes	blue	Su	N D	4	somewhat short-lived
Centaurea macrocephala	90cm/36in	leafy appearance	large yellow heads	Su	N D	3	
Centranthus ruber	70cm/28in	bluish green	red pink	Su	N D	5	also white form, seeds strongly
Crambe cordifolia	180cm/72in	large dark green	vast clouds of white	Esu	N D	6	leaves a gap after flowering
Dictamnus albus	80cm/32in	aromatic, divided	pink, white	Esu	N D	3	
Dierama pulcherrimum	100cm/40in	linear, large tufts	pink pendent bells	Su	M N D	8	
Eremurus stenophyllus	100cm/40in	rosette	pale yellow spires	Esu	D	5	magnificent plant
Eryngium planum	70cm/28in	basal rosettes	blue thistle heads	Su	N D	5	many other species
Geranium sanguineum	30cm/12in	divided, dark green	deep pink	Esu	N D	4	
Gypsophila paniculata	100cm/40in	greyish	huge clouds of white	Esu	N D	4	leaves a gap after flowering
Linaria purpurea	80cm/32in	erect, greyish	small purple	Su	N D	5	self-seeds
Morina longifolia	60cm/24in	spiny in rosette	whorls of white flowers	Esu	D	5	
Papaver orientale	80cm/32in	coarse hairy	large red poppies	Esu	N D	4	many cultivars available
Ruta graveolens	60cm/24in	neat grey foliage, E	small yellow	Su	N D	5	
Thermopsis villosa	120cm/48in	three-lobed leaves	yellow, lupin-like	Esu	N D	3	

ORNAMENTAL GRASSES

botanical name	height	foliage, habit	flower	season	situation	zone	remarks
Elymus arenarius	100cm/40in	blue-silver	grassy		N D	4	other species less invasive
Festuca glauca	30cm/12in	blue, tight tufts, E	uninteresting		N D	4	good value, many different forms
Helictotrichon sempervirens	100cm/40in	blue-green clumps	grassy	Esu	N D	4	
Koeleria glauca	30cm/12in	blue-green	tight fawn heads	Esu	D	4	
Pennisetum orientale	60cm/24in	grassy clumps	soft, mauvish	Su	N D	6	dislikes damp winters
Stipa gigantea	170cm/68in	large fine tufts	large, oat-like	Su	N D	6	one of the most dramatic grasses
Stipa pennata	80cm/32in	sparse, grassy	flowing, feathery	Esu	D	7	dislikes competition

Further reading

Ken Druse, *The Natural Habitat Garden*, Clarkson Potter, New York, 1994
Inspirational on plants native to the USA.

Hans Simon, *Grün ist Leben, BdB-Handbuch Wildstauden* (2 vols.), Pinneberg, 1992
One of the two best sources for of European wildflowers as garden plants.

Richard Hansen and Friedrich Stahl, *Perennials and their Garden Habitats*, Cambridge University Press, English translation, 1993
For reference and for an understanding of the philosophy of ecological planting.

Samuel B. Jones and Leonard E. Foote, *Gardening with Wildflowers*, Timber Press, Portland, 1993
The best of many practical books on growing North American wildflowers.

William Robinson, *The Wild Garden*, first published in 1870 and available in a facsimile edition from Century, London, 1993

Reinhard Witt, *Wildpflanzen für Jeden Garten*, BLV, Munich, 1994
Another excellent source on European wildflowers as garden plants.

Index

Page numbers in **bold** refer to the illustrations. *Italic* page numbers refer to the tables.

Hardiness zones

The hardiness zone ratings given for each plant in the tables suggest the appropriate minimum temperature a plant will tolerate in winter. The zone ratings are based on those devised by the United States Department of Agriculture. The chart on the right shows the annual average minimum temperature of each zone.

Zoning data can only be a rough guide. Hardiness depends on a great many factors, including the depth of a plant's roots, its water content at the onset of frost, the duration of cold weather, the force of the wind, and the length of, and temperatures encountered during, the preceding summer. Zone ratings given here are allocated to plants according to their tolerance of winter cold in the British Isles and Europe. In climates with hotter and/or drier summers, as in Australia and New Zealand, some plants will survive colder temperatures and their hardiness in these countries may occasionally be one, or even rarely two, zones lower than that quoted.

Most of the British Isles lies within Zone 8, with the exception of the western and southern coasts and central London, which are Zone 9, and the Highlands of Scotland, which are Zone 7.

CELSIUS	ZONES	°FAHRENHEIT
below −45	1	below −50
−45 to −40	2	−50 to −40
−40 to −34	3	−40 to −30
−34 to −29	4	−30 to −20
−29 to −23	5	−20 to −10
−23 to −18	6	−10 to 0
−18 to −12	7	0 to 10
−12 to −7	8	10 to 20
−7 to −1	9	20 to 30
−1 to 4	10	30 to 40
above 4	11	above 40

Acknowledgments

Author's acknowledgments

Researching this book involved a lot of travelling around to look at gardens in several different countries over a period of two years. This would have been impossible without the generosity of many people who gave me their time and who offered me hospitality, and I would like to take the opportunity to thank them. In particular I would like to mention the following: in Germany Urs Walser and Hans Simon showed and taught me much, and Reinhilde Frank put me up and drove me around for several days. In the Netherlands Rob Leopold organized a fantastic itinerary for me, whilst Theo den Dulk took me to many gardens in Arnhem. Piet and Anja Oudolf, whose inspirational work with perennials is very close to the approach outlined in this book, have also been generous with their hospitality, making my researches in the Netherlands that much easier and more enjoyable. I would also like to express my gratitude to two clients of mine, Jeremy Walsh and Sally Roberts who, having taken me on as a garden consultant, have found themselves thrust into the hurly-burly of the horticultural avant-garde. It is they who are enabling me to further my practical work in this dynamic and exciting area of gardening, and I am very grateful for their trust and support. I would also like to thank Jo Eliot for her constant love and interest in my work.

Photographic acknowledgments
t-top, b-below, l-left, r-right, m-middle, d-designer

Jan Den Hengst 19
Jerry Harpur 17, 34 (G. Keim and P. Wooster), 39 (Beth Chatto), 58-59, 60 (Great Dixter, East Sussex), 64r, 94 (d. Heide Stolpestad-Baldwin, Los Angeles, CA, USA), 106
Marijke Heuff 4-5 (Rene Ode, Holland), 6-7 and 14-15 (Ton ter Linden, Holland), 21 (Priona Gardens, Holland), 23 (Ton ter Linden, Holland), 24-25 (Westpark, Munich, Germany, d. Rosemary Weisse), 33 (Rene Ode, Holland), 36-37 and 43 (Ton ter Linden, Holland), 44-45 (d. Gilles Clement, France), 46t and 50 (Mr and Mrs van der Upwich, Holland), 54 (Sjef van der Molen, Holland), 56-57 (Ton ter Linden, Holland), 65 (Mrs L. Goossenaerts, Holland), 68-69 (Westpark, Munich, Germany, d. Rosemary Weisse), 72t and 72b (Ton ter Linden, Holland), 74 and 75 (Mr and Mrs de Visser, Holland), 76 (d. Wim Lasonder, Holland), 78 (Spijkerbuurt, Arnhem, Holland), 82-83 (Mrs L. Goossenaerts, Holland), 84 (d. Wim Lasonder, Holland), 85 (d. Gilles Clement, France), 87 and 90 (Ton ter Linden, Holland), 92-93 (Joseph Bayol, France), 95 and 103 (Westpark, Munich, Germany, d. Rosemary Weisse), 111 (de Heemtuin at Oostvoorne, Holland), 116 (Westpark, Munich, Germany, d. Rosemary Weisse), 123 (Ton ter Linden, Holland)
Saxon Holt 13 (Chanticleer Garden, Wayne, PA, USA), 30 (Roger Raiche, Berkeley, CA, USA), 31 (Ron Lutsko, Lafayette, CA, USA), 46b (Sally Cooke, MA, USA), 71, 131
Jacqui Hurst 47 (The Clock House, Wiltshire)
Noel Kingsbury 10 (Eastern Austrian Alps), 22 (Slovensky Raj National Park, Slovak Republic), 49 (Hermanshof, Weinheim, Germany, d. Urs Walser), 58 (Jan Jaap Boehle, Holland), 59 (Heimanshof Heemtuin, Hoofdorp, Holland, Tom Engelmann), 61 (Botanischer Garten Julius von Sachs Institut, Wurzburg, Germany), 62 (Dick van der Burg, Holland), 63 (Westpark, Munich, Germany, d. Rosemary Weisse), 66 and 67 (d. Dr Hans Simon, Germany), 70 (Hermanshof, Weinheim, Germany, d. Urs Walser), 89 (Joop and Greet Atsma, Holland), 100l (Westpark, Munich, Germany, d. Rosemary Weisse), 100r (Botanischer Garten Julius von Sachs Institut, Wurzburg, Germany), 101b (Westpark, Munich, Germany, d. Rosemary Weisse), 119br (Cowley Manor Gardens, Glos.), 120, 121t, 121b, 127 (Rene Ode, Holland), 151r
Andrew Lawson 1, 9 (Hermanshof, Weinheim, Germany, d. Urs Walser), 18, 27, 29 (Hermanshof, Weinheim, Germany, d. Urs Walser), 35 and 38 (Westpark, Munich, Germany, d. Rosemary Weisse), 40 and 42(Hermanshof, Weinheim, Germany, d. Urs Walser), 64l, 79 (Westpark, Munich, Germany, d. Rosemary Weisse), 81(Planting by Miriam Rothschild at Chatsworth, Derbyshire), 96 and 101t (Hermanshof, Weinheim, Germany, d. Rosemary Weisse), 129, 134, 135, 140, 141, 146, 147, 150, 151l
Clive Nichols 26 (The Anchorage, Kent), 52 (The Dower House, Glos.), 88 (Wolfson College, Oxford)
Elizabeth Rodgers 53 (Catherine Hull, MA, USA)
Gary Rogers 20
Elizabeth Whiting & Associates/Karl Dietrich Buhler 115t
Jeff Wookey © FLL 104-5, 108, 109, 112-114, 115bl and br, 119t, m, and bl, 124-126
Steven Wooster 2-3 and 98-99 (Beth Chatto), 102

Publishers' acknowledgments
The publishers are grateful to Studio Gossett for their initial design work. Thanks are also due to Sally Launder for her watercolour plans, to Hilary Bird for the index and to Sally Cracknell, Margherita Gianni, Maggi McCormack, Annabel Morgan and Patti Taylor for their assistance in producing the book.

Horticultural Consultants Tony Lord, Antonia Johnson, John Elseley

Project Editor Caroline Bugler
Editors Sarah Mitchell, Penny David
Assistant Editor James Bennett
Art Editor Patricia Going
Picture Editor Anne Fraser
Production Kim van Woerkom
Editorial Director Erica Hunningher
Art Director Caroline Hillier